I0464737

Other Published Works by Jack Sutherland

Put Time on Your Side
How to Achieve Financial Independence in Retirement

Time to Catch Up
Powerful Strategies to Accelerate Retirement Funding

INVESTING 1.0.1 WITH PURPOSE

Taking the Mystery Out of Investing

JACK SUTHERLAND

 iUniverse®

INVESTING 1.0.1 WITH PURPOSE
TAKING THE MYSTERY OUT OF INVESTING

Copyright © 2018 Jack Sutherland.

All rights reserved. No part of this book may be used or reproduced by any means, graphic, electronic, or mechanical, including photocopying, recording, taping or by any information storage retrieval system without the written permission of the author except in the case of brief quotations embodied in critical articles and reviews.

iUniverse books may be ordered through booksellers or by contacting:

iUniverse
1663 Liberty Drive
Bloomington, IN 47403
www.iuniverse.com
1-800-Authors (1-800-288-4677)

Because of the dynamic nature of the Internet, any web addresses or links contained in this book may have changed since publication and may no longer be valid. The views expressed in this work are solely those of the author and do not necessarily reflect the views of the publisher, and the publisher hereby disclaims any responsibility for them.

Any people depicted in stock imagery provided by Getty Images are models, and such images are being used for illustrative purposes only. Certain stock imagery © Getty Images.

ISBN: 978-1-5320-5701-4 (sc)
ISBN: 978-1-5320-5702-1 (e)

Library of Congress Control Number: 2018911234

Print information available on the last page.

iUniverse rev. date: 09/21/2018

Investing 1.0.1 With Purpose

is

Dedicated to
Our son

Mark

For his insightful questions about how to make
long-term investment decisions.

CONTENTS

THE GREAT SEDUCTION[1]

The people who created this country built a moral structure around money. The Puritan legacy inhibited luxury and self-indulgence. Benjamin Franklin spread a practical gospel that emphasized hard work, temperance, and frugality. Millions of parents, preachers, newspaper editors, and teachers expounded the message. The result was quite remarkable.

The United States has been an affluent nation since its founding. But the country was, by and large, not corrupted by wealth. For centuries, it remained industrious, ambitious, and frugal.

Over the past 30 years, much of that has been shredded. The social norms and institutions that encouraged frugality and spending what you earn have been undermined. The institutions that encourage debt and living for the moment have been strengthened. The country's moral guardians are forever looking for decadence out of Hollywood and reality TV. But the most rampant decadence today is financial decadence, the trampling of decent norms about how to use and harness money.

David Brooks
THE NEW YORK TIMES
June 10, 2008

---

[1] *Enough,* by John C. Bogel, John Wiley & Sons, Inc, 2009,opening page

INTRODUCTION

Congratulations on acquiring your personal copy of *Investing 1.0.1 with Purpose!* Statistically, you belong to a relatively small group of individuals who either want to get started investing or who want to improve on their existing poor investment discipline and performance. You are looking for some new perspectives and ideas by reading this book. To be a successful investor, it starts with taking the mystery out of investing.

My entire career has involved working in finance. As a banker, I worked with small businesses and their owner families in helping them achieve their financial goals. This work included structuring loans to provide acquisition capital or construction loans to expand the business or working capital lines of credit for everyday business cash flow needs. It usually involved getting the owner families to work with our banks' wealth management team to assist them in succession planning, retirement and estate planning and employee benefit plan design. My lifetime of financial experience, combined with my Masters of Business Administration (MBA), private business ownership and personal retirement planning development can benefit everyday investors by bringing a unique focus to the strategies outlined in this book. I can assist you in achieving a secure retirement plan.

In some of my presentations I ask people when was the last time they read a book about investing and if they can remember the title? Fewer than 20 percent usually respond affirmatively to both questions. You are a unique individual by having taken the initiative to pursue some of the action steps necessary to create success in investing. You are a member of the elite, top one-fifth, twentieth percent (20%), of individual investors!

The American dream of owning a home, being financially capable of sending your children to college and retiring with a comfortable lifestyle are at risk. This risk has been magnified by the dramatic paradigm shift of who is responsible for your personal retirement plan. The days of your employer providing a fully funded pension plan that gave assurances of a lifetime income are a relic of the past for most Americans. Company provided 401(k) plans (called defined contribution plans) have replaced those defined benefit pension plans of old. Each individual has now assumed the responsibility for his or her own retirement plans. Ignoring this reality will create a looming retirement crisis.

Yes, the model is broken! The days of attending college or trade school, graduating and finding a full time job (remember the rise of the new "gig" economy) that provides a pension benefit at retirement are gone forever. This is why *you* are the only person accountable and responsible for *your* retirement planning.

I introduce a concept called financial wellness, as one way to better prepare individuals for one of the largest financial challenges they will face as adults. Financial wellness is more than financial literacy. It encompasses financial literacy as well as the need for learning other basic financial skills about how to manage money, fund emergency savings accounts, develop and follow budgets and reducing debt. I believe attending financial education seminars is a good use of your time. Providing for your retirement should also be an important topic of these financial wellness seminars. Financial wellness should become a lifelong pursuit.

American workers have shown they can carry life's stresses into the workplace. These various stress levels may affect productivity, ability to maintain focus on critical and time sensitive issues, as well as an employee's ultimate willingness to retire when offered a buyout package or when normal retirement age occurs.

Both mental and physical health may be affected by money worries. Seek financial wellness as an antidote to these stresses and worries. Some financial wellness instruction may include other topics than those mentioned above. The important thing is to access this training either through your employer or on your own. This is very important for your future.

Investing 1.0.1 with Purpose is a content-rich message of hope for the future. It is a compilation of proven, understandable and workable investing strategies for the everyday investor. These strategies can assist you along the journey toward becoming a believer in, as well as a motivated prophet of, the value of long term investing. I will highlight a low risk investment strategy that may help you achieve many of your personal investment goals. In today's changed workplace, managing money may be as important as earning it. Make today the day you begin to take charge of your financial future.

In addition to offering a sensible framework to increase the probability of achieving investment success, this book outlines tested investment approaches that can help reduce the personal stress level often encountered by first time, non-seasoned investors. *Investing 1.0.1 with Purpose* has encompassed and transcended both goals, almost beyond definition.

Over the course of your working years, building wealth to achieve long-term goals can be segmented into three phases. Phase I is basic savings and investing. Phase II involves being able to hold on to these investments while competing interests from self gratification purchases pummel you on a regular basis. Finally, Phase III is the retirement phase when you will need to develop a plan for spending wisely to make your nest egg last. This is all about managing your withdrawal rate and other major expenditures. Most of us need assistance to perform well in all three phases of wealth building.

With baby boomers now swelling the ranks of the retired, or soon to be retired, the market for financial advice is booming. Do you need to pay for this advice or is it possible for everyday investors to develop an individual plan on their own for a secure retirement? I will help you answer these questions.

I have formatted this book in four easy to read sections. Part I shares the background you need to prepare for some changes you will need to make to move forward with this life changing activity. Part II covers the fundamentals of successful investing. Part III will help you overcome some of the major obstacles standing between you and committing to long term investing. Finally, Part IV showcases some of the lifelong benefits you can expect from having implemented these investment strategies.

Like many readers, some early mistakes and misguided ideas about the process of building wealth for the future may be the cause of your deferred action on the idea of getting started in providing for your retirement. It is never too late to recover from prior, financial setbacks!

I am attempting to change human behavior. It is a difficult task and efforts to modify behavior always run the risk of failure. The powerful human trait of inertia remains one of the most influential forces in financial decision-making. Inertia holds you back from moving forward. Break the restraints of inertia! If you are willing to work, spend time learning about a few investment strategies, mold them to your unique circumstances while maintaining financial discipline, this can be your lifelong financial guidebook to achieving financial independence.

My over riding principle in writing *Investing 1.0.1 with Purpose* is based on following the basic rules of commonsense. One of the key factors in getting everyday investors to save more for retirement and other financial goals is to make the process as easy as possible. More than half of American workers may not have enough in retirement savings to maintain their standard of living later in life, according to an estimate from the Center for Retirement Research at Boston College. This needs to change.

The best time to get started is now. *Investing 1.0.1 with Purpose* was written for you.

The only person you can trust to secure a well-funded retirement plan is yourself. No one really cares if you fail at retirement but you will be delighted with your success.

As Americans, we all enjoy many freedoms that come with our citizenship. The ability to enjoy freedom of choice can be both a burden and a blessing. It forces us to take responsibility for our individual actions. We have no one else to blame for our inaction. The choice is yours!

I hope, as an everyday investor, you do not fall victim to the statement "I wish I had read this book earlier in my career." You can avoid this result for others by reading *Investing1.0.1 with Purpose* now and using it as a call to action on how to improve on building wealth for the future. After you have read this book, pass it along to someone who might benefit from the same advice.

You may be curious why the title of this book includes the numbers 1.0.1. These numbers are used for a very specific reason. Just like many software updates and upgrades use a similar numbering system, *Investing 1.0.1 with Purpose* represents a major upgrade to each everyday investors approach to building wealth for the future. Within *Investing 1.0.1 with Purpose*, each number delineated by a period represents a single, separate component of a plan to achieve your various pre-determined investment purposes. A focus on long-term investing, low costs and a broad, diversified portfolio will ultimately be the keys to your success.

Advice is one of those things that is easier to give than to receive. If you can accept the basic concept that you are openly seeking help in understanding and improving your investment returns, then the essence of the advice within this book will have been received. I hope you will refer to these recommendations often as you travel the road of taking the mystery out of investing.

"The investor's chief problem –
and even his worst enemy –
is likely to be himself."

Benjamin Graham
The Father of Value Investing

PART I

BACKGROUND

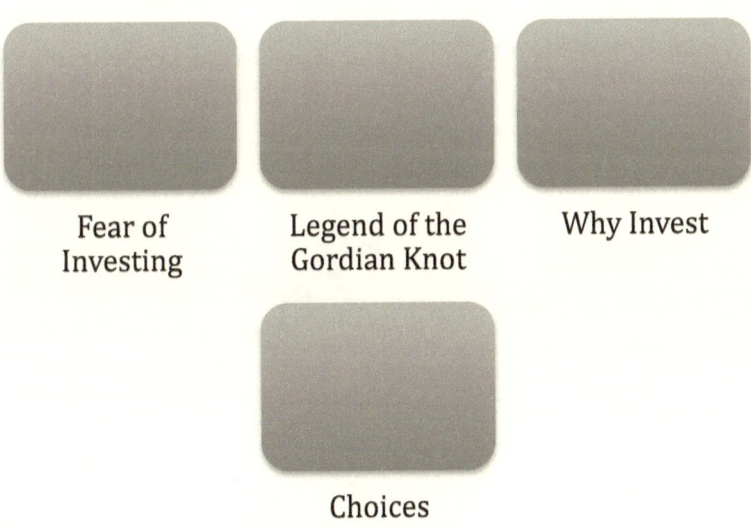

Fear of
Investing

Legend of the
Gordian Knot

Why Invest

Choices

FEAR OF INVESTING

Some 30 years ago, my friend, I will call her Maria, asked my financial advice about starting a retirement plan. I introduced her to several investment concepts and recommended she begin her initial stock market experience with a few conservative investment selections. After our first consultation, Maria told me she was not comfortable putting her hard earned money at risk in the stock market. After probing for a better understanding of her decision, she said she was too intimidated by the strange vocabulary, unique phrases and rambling explanations of the investment process. She believed investing was the same as gambling. She chose to make no decision about her retirement plan for now, which was a decision in itself. Taking no action is always a default decision.

Over time, Maria invested the majority of her investable funds in rental real estate. She was able to paint, do minor repairs and manage her real estate by herself or with help from her children for many years. Now, with the children educated and gone from the house, she is of the age where she hires most of the property management details from an outside source. This additional cost reduces her total return from her rental properties.

Maria is one of the most honest, hard working individuals I know. She has always been a saver, finding a way to put away a little from whatever income she had. She took the risks of borrowing money through real estate mortgages to invest in rental properties. She built her property portfolio to include four rental houses. She did not understand the additional risk of concentrating her investments in one asset class like rental real estate. To her credit though, she invested in what she understood. She will never make up for the lost opportunities she missed in the stock market over those 30 years, but fortunately, her rental real estate properties have shown nice appreciation during these past few decades, along with providing regular, monthly cash flow.

Years had passed from our initial conversation about her retirement plans. She contacted me again to let me know she had done some reading and other research and decided to begin to save for retirement through her company's 401(k) plan. I was very supportive of this decision. I helped her make some initial selections from the various investment options offered by the plan. She began with investing enough from her salary to meet the matching threshold from her employer. I encouraged her to also open a traditional Individual Retirement Account (IRA) and to fund it with $100.00 per month, after making the initial minimum deposit to open the account. I am pleased to report these two retirement accounts have performed very well for Maria over time. The combination of income producing real estate and her 401(k) and IRA investments have given Maria a nice diversification of assets for retirement.

As I thought about Maria and her reasons for not making an initial decision about investing in the market, I realized there are a lot of Maria's who are intimidated by the stock market. They avoid one of the most prolific wealth building tools available out of fear, anxiety and uncertainty.

This book is about more than financial literacy; it is about taking the mystery out of investing and promoting overall financial wellness. It is about explaining the stock market and simplifying several investment strategies in such a way as to encourage more participation from individuals whose comfort level is lacking when it comes to investing. The stock market remains one of the most proven ways to build wealth over time for future needs such as retirement, purchase a home, and buy a car or to accumulate funds for a college education.

The fear of investing held by some everyday investors may have been further exacerbated by the real time closing of Bear Stearns over a decade ago. The demise of this major Wall Street firm in 2008, along with others such as Lehman Brothers and the urgent need for Merrill Lynch to be absorbed by Bank of America, caused a significant public loss of trust and confidence in the stock markets. Ultimately, Bear Stearns was forced to seek a buyer and was sold to JPMorgan Chase. Bear had been a major participant in the subprime mortgage business. Seeing these major Wall Street companies fail drove fear and loss of trust among everyday investors.

Fear can be real or perceived, but once trust is broken, it is hard to regain. Fear can be based on real events like the failure of Bear Stearns or it can be based on a fear of the future or the unknown. Fear based on real events is rational while fear based on the future may be irrational. It has been said that, "Fear of the future is nothing more than fear of the past." This is manifested by an anxiety over the repeat of past, negative events. This is a natural response to any threat that could be real or only perceived. In either case the fear is real.

Hard as it may be, maintaining a rational approach to long-term wealth building is a must. Avoiding decisions based on emotional knee jerk reactions to economic events will provide a sound footing for you to implement an investment plan with purpose.

If investing were easy, there would be no need for books like this. The one phrase that best describes the investment process and simultaneously strikes fear in the minds of many is *Caveat Emptor*, a Latin phrase roughly translated to mean, "Let the buyer beware." Other common language appearing in most investment marketing materials is phrases like "Not FDIC Insured. No Bank Guarantee. May Lose Value."

This is enough warning that it may scare away everyday investors. It is like all the side effects listed for certain medications. The potential side effects sound so onerous, whom, in their right mind, would take the risk of using those medications?

Yet for most, those same medications, when properly prescribed and directions followed, offer benefits and healing to the patient. The same can be said for investing.

Any investment has risks; this book is about mitigating those risks through education and developing a plan of action with purpose. This approach has a proven record of success over the past two decades. Fear should never play a role. "Always maintain a healthy respect for the market" might be better than the Latin phrase cited earlier.

The lack of knowledge and understanding of the investment markets can scare everyday investors into a paralysis, where no action is taken to address the future financial needs of their family. Sometimes a market correction of 10% or more in a drop in the valuation of the stock market can cause extreme caution to replace confidence. FDIC insured safe products like a bank savings account will not produce enough growth needed to fund a secure retirement.

This is not an acceptable outcome. Neither is relying solely on social security or a company pension plan, if one is available. Neither of these financial support systems can provide for future financial security on a stand-alone basis. Most company pension plans, known as defined benefit plans, have gone the way of the flip phone. There are a few of them still functioning in the marketplace, but their remaining years of continued service are in question. Fear of investing is normal.

As human beings, we tend to live life best when we are in a forward mode of thinking. On the other hand, understanding life usually only occurs when we are in a rearview or backward reflection mode. The quiet time of reflection seems to offer us a clear 20-20 perspective. Unfortunately, at this reflective stage, it may be too late to effectively accumulate adequate funding for your retirement or other larger, financial goals.

Using hindsight as a way to obtain a clearer understanding of life and past decisions always seems like an excuse for failure, it seems to me. Hindsight can illuminate your lack of commitment to an idea or a course of action.

- Failure to take action
- Failure to change behavior
- Failure to accept the fact you are the only one responsible for planning and funding your retirement
- Failure to think beyond today
- Failure to mold your financial future exactly as you want it to be
- Failure to plan equates to planning for failure.

You really have three choices when it comes to investing: hire professional help or do-it-yourself. A third option is to use a hybrid of the first two choices by dividing your investments into one fund to be managed professionally and another fund that you manage yourself. In all three of these scenarios some investment research and time spent understanding the markets is required. Any combination of these methods of investing can work for you. The only question is which one is the optimal choice?

This book is written for a very broad audience, including late stage baby boomers, millennials, and any other investor looking for different perspectives and new ideas, as well as individuals over the age of 50 who are confronting the reality of retirement head-on. For them time may have become their enemy, as the remaining time is too short?

Sadly, many people will not attain financial security in retirement. The temptation is far too great to spend now rather than live below their income and invest for their future. This is where financial wellness and financial literacy meet at the intersection of financial discipline, or the lack of discipline. I do not want you to be part of that group of retirees who suffer financial anxiety in retirement.

I am interested in helping those who want to help themselves. Financial opportunities are well within reach for most Americans. If you are willing to work and set aside money for any future goal, I can help you achieve your goals. The past is fixed in place but the future is not. We all learn by experience and both bad and good behavioral traits can be acquired. Let's focus on the good traits of investing. It is time to take the mystery out of investing by balancing the risks and potential rewards.

Risk and Reward are Related

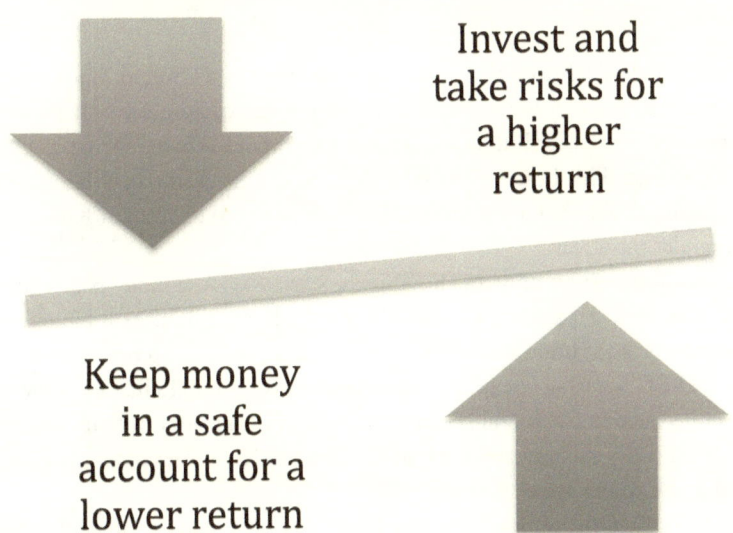

Invest and take risks for a higher return

Keep money in a safe account for a lower return

CHAPTER

LEGEND OF THE GORDIAN KNOT[2]

There is a classical story that legend tells us involved a knotted rope tied in multiple layers and was so complicated that no man could untie it. If anyone were successful, according to the legend, they would become the next ruler of all of Asia. This is according to Arrian, an ancient historian. Many tried and many failed. The only successful man to solve the Gordian Knot was Alexander the Great.

He didn't try to untie the knot in the same way as so many before him had attempted. He drew his sword and cut the knot in half! As it fell to the ground, the knot unraveled. Alexander the Great went on to rule Asia from 331-323 BC, creating one of the largest land mass empires in history. He was never defeated in battle and is considered one of the greatest military leaders in all of history, all because he solved the Gordian Knot. Alexander the Great died at the young age of 32.

Since then the phrase "Gordian Knot" has been used as a metaphor for solving any extremely difficult and involved problem by thinking creatively. Today, we call that process thinking outside the box.

For those of you less familiar with classical history, let me briefly explain the difference between a legend and a myth. A legend is presumed to have

---

[2] The four sources of the Legend of the Gordian Knot are given in Robin Lane Fox. *Alexander the Great (19730 1986:* notes to Chapter 10), p.518; Fox recounts the anecdote, pp149-151

a basis in historical fact. A myth is nothing more than fanciful story telling without any basis in facts. The story of the Gordian Knot is a legend. Need I say more?

I do not want you to feel all tied up in knots when it comes to the topic of investing. There are so many advisors bombarding you from TV, radio, print and social media about how difficult it is to make money in the stock and bond markets. Their approach seems to be based on how to make the process "the more difficult the better" when it comes to any investing concept. This approach makes it impossible for the everyday investor to make sense out of these various sales promotions. These advisors hope if they make investing so complicated, you will have no choice but to hire them and pay their fees to guide you in the creation of an investment portfolio. You are too smart to fall for these raw tactics. Do not be alarmed! There is no need for worry, as there are alternative investment solutions available for you.

This is what I want you to accomplish. I want you to have the self-confidence that you can solve the saving and investment problems of everyday investors by learning about and applying the strategies outlined in this book. This will help unravel the "Gordian Knot" of investing for you. I will do this by demystifying the investment process, bring clarity to the confusing terms and simplifying vocabulary by applying a common sense approach to providing for your financial future. Whether you decide to use professional financial advisors or do-it-yourself is your decision. I do not care which path you take, I just want you to arrive at the same destination of a well-funded retirement plan. Either approach can result in solid, long-term financial wealth building.

Wall Street has called small dollar, everyday investors part of the "dumb money?" Really! Is this because some individual investors make mistakes when they are guided by their emotions rather than following a well-devised, fact-based investment plan? History is full of stories about investors of all ages who sold low and bought high (the exact opposite of what successful, long term investors do) or who make the fatal mistake of going to all cash just before the market took off on an incredible and extended rise in valuation. When you hear the occasional story of the individual investor who sold everything and went to cash just before the market had a major correction, it is the equivalent of the individual gambler telling you about his big winnings from his last trip to Las Vegas. What about all the times he/she suffered loses? Those stories about losses do not seem to ever be told?

I do not believe everyday investors are "dumb money". You can become part of the "smart money" crowd, if you follow a simple plan that includes:

- Always invest with a plan and purpose
- Stay the course and do not let emotions rule your decision making
- Stay fully invested, no matter what happens in the market
- Avoid frequent trading activity, as this adds to the cost of investing
- Be content to match market returns and avoid taking greater risks trying to beat the market

Predicting and/or modifying human behavior is more difficult than predicting earthquakes, tornados or hurricanes. As Sir Isaac Newton is reputed to have said, he "could calculate the motions of the heavenly bodies, but not the madness of the people." *Investing 1.0.1 with Purpose* is about modifying your financial behavior.

In October 2017 American Richard Thaler won the Nobel Prize in economics for upending the idea that individuals make rational decisions about their future financial wellbeing. Dr. Richard Thaler, Ph.D., an economics professor with the University of Chicago Booth School of Business, helped to advance the concept of automatic enrollment in retirement accounts like 401(k) plans and making automatic increases in contributions to these plans over time. Dr. Thaler is a pioneer in the area of behavioral economics. His research has built a bridge of understanding between economics and psychology.

Dr. Thaler's research has shown that an individual's financial behavior is largely a problem of faulty or lack of self-control. Additionally, he documented that people will save more for retirement, if you take some of the effort out of it.

Why are Dr. Richard Thaler's research findings important to everyday investors? He and his research assistants hypothesized, for example, that the reason stocks that performed poorly over the past three years tended to eventually bounce back more rapidly is that people were prone to "overreact" to unexpected and dramatic news events. This over reaction drove valuations lower than the facts might indicate. In turn, this insight gives everyday investors the power to bring a more rational behavior to investing.

Remembering to exercise this insight in every investment decision is the challenge.

Think rationally, not emotionally. I know it is easier said than done. Think of financial discipline along with personal commitment as the two cornerstones of your new investing model. The virtue of self-discipline does not come naturally to human beings. Remove or at least control emotions when making long-term investment decisions. I acknowledge this is not an easy task. As human beings, it is impossible to remove 100% of your emotions from decision-making. Being aware of the destructive power of emotion driven investing and controlling these instincts as best you can, will put you ahead of the pack of other investors stuck in the rut of simply following their gut instincts.

The strategies outlined in this book are based, to a very limited extent, on the research and published findings of economist Dr. Richard Thaler's insights in explaining irrational behavior in the market. I applaud his research and believe in keeping the investing process as simple as possible. A more rational approach to long-term investing as proposed in *Investing 1.0.1 with Purpose* should improve an everyday investors probability for success.

The Gordian Knot of investing can be untied for you and for others with this robust, non-emotional approach to building wealth for the future. Make this the beginning of your family legend about successful investing.

Unravel the Investment Process, Step by Step, to Build Wealth for the Future

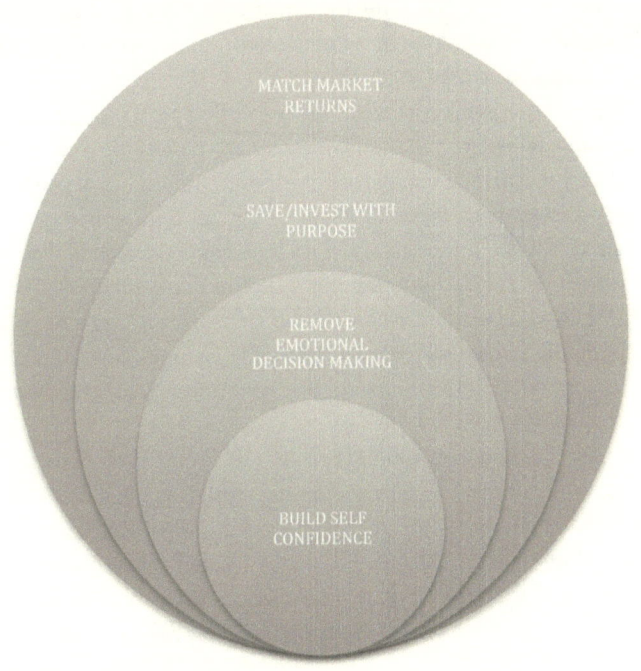

3

WHY INVEST

What does it mean to invest? It means to save or put aside funds to be used for building future wealth. Sounds very straightforward. How can you afford to do this while working and covering the expenses inherent in raising a family? I will show you in later chapters how to do both: support your family and set aside savings for the future.

Telling you that it takes savings first before you have funds available for investing is like telling you the sun comes up every morning and sets in the evening. Everyone already knows that fact. So why do so many people avoid saving? My answer is they are all about consumption, living paycheck-to-paycheck and just live for today. Until you overcome the lack of saving, you will not move forward in beginning the wealth building process.

I will show you later how to get started saving by making a few changes in your daily life. These will not be draconian changes, just a little tweak here and there in the choices you make everyday in how and when you spend money.

In reality, building wealth could become a purpose in and of itself. When is having enough money adequate to stop saving? For some, it never seems to be enough? After all, that is apparently what some of the wealthiest men seem to believe. Think Warren Buffett, Bill Gates and Jeff Bezos, to name a few. These are three of the wealthiest men in America. Amassing a fortune should not be, however, the final goal of investing for everyday investors. It should only be the process used to arrive at a better place in your life in the future. I am more focused on your ability to build future wealth for the benefit of your family, not just accumulating money for the sake of having a large nest egg balance.

"For most of us, as it is said, *enough* is a $1 more than you need." [3]

There really is no need to invest just for the sake of investing unless your goal is to become the richest scrooge on the block. Investing without purpose or multiple purposes is like baking a cake without anyone to eat and enjoy the result of your baking prowess. Other idle thoughts about investing without purpose:

- It is like driving around all day without a destination
- It is like building a house and not finishing the roof
- It is like waking up in the morning with nothing on your agenda for the entire day; do you waste the day or do you do something constructive

What is an investment objective? This is the fundamental reason you are investing. Like other priorities, investment objectives change over time. The second question is to decide how you will invest in any or all of the three basic asset categories:

- Risk free – cash, cash equivalents and short-term US Treasuries (1-5 year maturities and Treasury bills)
- Core Investments – Stocks, funds, ETFs and Bonds
- Alternative investments-Real Estate, Commodities, Options, Art and Coins

For now, let's just focus on risk free and core investments. Risk free is any cash asset or FDIC insured deposit or US government note or bond. Within these two categories are sub-categories called asset classes. Core investments consist of domestic stock, exchange traded funds, international stock, large cap, small cap, corporate bonds, US Treasuries and many other different asset classes. Ultimately, deciding on an asset allocation among the asset classes will influence the total return of your investment portfolio. We will get into these details later.

---

[3] *Enough*, by John C. Bogel, John Wiley & Sons, Inc, 2009, p238

To return to my original metaphor, when you add purpose to investing, for instance to buy a home or save money to send your kids to college or to provide for your retirement, it is the same as having a hungry family sitting around the dining room table waiting to enjoy the warm cake as it comes out of the oven. I can see their smiles now, as they savor the smell of the baking and the taste of the cake. I also envision you enjoying the new home or bursting with pride in the child who has earned a college degree or you entering retirement with a financially secure future.

My overwhelming recommendation is for you to consider investing in the US stock and bond (fixed income) markets. Recent studies have shown just over 50% of adult Americans own stock. Some buy individual shares and mutual funds while others participate in the markets only through their 401(k) plans. To address the looming retirement crisis, a larger number of everyday investors need to get more involved in the market.

My reasoning is very simple. Over the past 100 years, the Dow Jones Industrial Average (DJIA) has averaged 5.7% annual returns. Where else can you find such a consistent performance over an extended period of time?

Today, where are the alternatives for setting aside funds to be invested for the future? Have you recently looked at the interest rates banks are offering for savings accounts and certificates of deposit? These rates are so low they do not even cover the current inflation rate. The current interest rates are the lowest I have seen in my adult life. So you need to find somewhere else to place your investment funds, if you are to achieve growth. Many alternatives exist like stocks, bonds, mutual funds, exchange traded funds, real estate, corporate bonds, government bonds, private investments and others.

Just to give you a sampling of the annual returns for a few selected indexes or mutual funds, look at these one-year performance numbers, as of December 31, 2017.

One-Year Returns

- S&P 500 Index 19.4%
- Dow Jones Industrial Average 25.1%
- Vanguard Total Intl Index (VGTSX) 27.4%
- Vanguard Total Intl Bond Fund-Admiral 3.6%
- SPDR S&P 500 ETF (SPY) 21.7%
- Vanguard Total Stock Market (ETF) 21.2%

Source: The Wall Street Journal

These performance numbers are unmatched with most other investment opportunities with similar risks.

Soaring stock prices during 2017 have driven stock valuations to new records. Caution is needed to avoid becoming euphoric about these prices without the underlying supporting data in the form of growing company earnings, continued low inflation and a new, revised tax law that, hopefully, will deliver on the promise of increased economic growth throughout the country. The tax reform bill signed in late December 2017 is the largest tax law change in the USA in decades. The outlook for 2018 and beyond is encouraging on all of these data points.

Warren Buffett is considered one of the most successful, long-term investors in the world. He is the CEO of Berkshire Hathaway Inc., a diversified investment company, headquartered in Omaha, Nebraska. The Class A common shares (symbol BRK-A) are the most expensive individual shares traded on the NYSE. Recent pricing was $295,000 per share! From the 2017 annual report of Berkshire Hathaway:

"Investing is an activity in which consumption today is foregone in an attempt to allow greater consumption at a later date. "Risk" is the possibility that this objective won't be attained."

Warren Buffett

We talk about the risks of investing but there is also a risk of not investing. That risk manifests itself through the concept of something you do not know can cost you money. The cost is in lost opportunity and ultimately having your funds become trapped in a low rate, low return scenario during your working years. Those working years should be some of the peak saving years. You may think this could not be the result of safe, prudent investments in bank certificates of deposit and other FDIC insured products. This is a false sense of security that will not reach the wealth-building threshold you desire.

Insured bank deposits are a good holding area to accumulate funds for future investing. They also provide a safe source of liquidity. They may not grow to the amount needed to fund your retirement over a 25-30 year period because of the low rates of interest offered on such products. Remember the proven relationship potential between risk and reward.

You may recall the old adage "You have to spend money to make money." My revised version of this phrase is "you have to invest money to build wealth." The only other way to legally accumulate wealth is through inheritance. Most of us are not so fortunate as to have a large sum of money pass to us from our parents or relatives. Therefore, it is important to learn about investing, if you hope to build a secure financial life to fund your retirement.

The need to build financial security necessitates each of us to engage in the process of wealth building. I do not use the phrase "to become rich" as the word rich is a relative term. It has different meanings for every reader. Rich also can have a negative connotation as a class differentiator, as between middle class and rich, or the rich upper 1%. This is not the intent of this book. I do not want to divide everyday investors into narrowly defined categories but, rather, be all-inclusive in this message about wealth building. I want you to build wealth to provide for yourself and your family and not become a financial burden on other family members or society at large when you retire.

There exists a serious gap, call it the longevity gap[4] or statistical chasm, in our projected planning horizon. This longevity gap or chasm is the difference between what Social Security estimates how long you will live and the reality of your lifespan. Starting at age 50, Social Security estimates the average American male will live until age 80 and the average female will live to age 83. At a person's actual age of 65, that same source projects lifespan of a male extends to 84.3 years and 88.6 for a female. These are the projected average ages for all Americans.

You are one-of-a-kind! You are a unique individual with your own genetic code and life expectancy. Meaningful investment advice should be person specific. The many positive reasons to invest can be generically applied but the actual results in reality will depend on your life span.

People in the upper income brackets may tend to live longer than those with average or lower incomes. Some of this difference may be based on type of career, access to healthcare or the ability to access medical specialists, as needed. People today seem to be living healthier lifestyles and living longer. Managing a healthy lifestyle is very person specific.

---

[4] Longevity gap is a term coined by Jane Bryant Quinn, the financial journalist and a leading commentator on personal finance.

My mother lived to age 104, remaining in good health until she fell and broke her hip. She remained of sound mind up until the end. I can only hope I have inherited her genes for a similar long life? You need to plan for living longer than what Social Security projects. You will need to bridge this built-in longevity gap or chasm. Expect to live into your mid 90's, as it is well within your reach. I am convinced people should be more worried about living too long rather than dying too young.

There is another way to consider this difference in projected versus actual lifespan. Think about how to cover the difference financially of how long you expect to live and the projection of living 25-30 years after full retirement age (FRA 67). This will bring the longevity gap into a sharper focus. If you have only $25,000 in retirement savings at full retirement age, you are woefully underfunded. I have read some studies that found a large number of people had more in debt than retirement savings when they reached full retirement age. These types of scenarios have the makings for a severe and ugly unresolved retirement crisis.

In my previous books, *Put Time on Your Side* and *Time to Catch Up,* I spent considerable time discussing the positive power of compound interest. Time is the most important variable in the formula for compound interest. I am not going to repeat those paragraphs here. Suffice it to say, the longer you can invest and leave invested funds working for you, the better your financial security in retirement. Compound interest can be your best friend. The sooner you get started, the better and more meaningful the relationship becomes. I do not want your working years to become a poignant reminder of the passing of time and lost opportunities.

I will not be drawn into the debate about whether stocks are overvalued, undervalued or if and when the market will undergo a major correction (correction defined as a 10% or more drop in prices or market valuation). The reality is no one can predict the market. The best time to enter the market is now, if you are a serious long-term investor. Trying to time the market is nothing but a fool's game. Staying fully invested over a long period of years is a proven way to build wealth. Daily, weekly, monthly, quarterly and annual market fluctuations should not be of major concern when you are a committed long-term investor.

I repeat, you must find a way to bridge this gap in your projected versus actual lifespan. Stuffing money in the mattress or socking it away in a bank savings account will not get the job done. One solution might be in changing the allocation in your portfolio between stocks and bonds. Perhaps a higher percentage in stocks and a lower percentage in bonds as you age may be one part of the solution. This change would also increase your risk profile. This would be a more aggressive allocation that might challenge your risk tolerance. Another answer to bridging this longevity gap is to save more money.

I am convinced you must be invested in the stock market to achieve financial security, unless you have special expertise in real estate or some other niche asset category. Lacking any such special expertise, participation in the financial markets is one of the best ways for everyday investors to build wealth.

Investing is one way to put your money where your mouth is IF you believe the USA and the global economy will grow and prosper over the next 10-20-30 years. Being in the stock market is one of the best ways for everyday investors to participate in this future growth.

What about alternative investments like real estate, commodities, options, art, rare coins or oil and gas producing properties? With the exception of real estate, I would avoid these other types of investment. As everyday investors, you may lack the specialized knowledge needed to properly evaluate the risks associated with these alternative investments. Income producing real estate, on the other hand, may fit into some everyday investors portfolio through the purchase of individual properties or through publically traded real estate investment trusts (REIT). REIT investments offer some diversification among different properties while typically paying out a high yield. Whether to include some real estate in your portfolio or not is your decision.

It is your responsibility to find a way to minimize the delta between your vision of retirement and the reality of your lifestyle in the future. No one can do this for you, as you are in-charge of both variables: your vision of the future and your current and future lifestyle. You should not enter retirement with crushed hopes for the future. Retirement should be a liberating phase of your life; enjoyment and time spent with those you love is how you should want to spend this later stage of life.

The personal US savings rate as of December 2017 was 2.4%. This rate is defined as savings as a share of after tax income. The 2.4% rate is down from a high of 10.0% and has been declining the past few years based on research by the Commerce Department from 2005-2017. With Americans saving less and borrowing more, this does not bode well for their personal financial future.

The savings rate of 2.4% is the lowest in the past 12 years. This low rate may be indicative that many are feeling the benefit of rising asset values, like the stock market and home values. They are comfortable spending more as a result of what economists call the "wealth effect." If this trend continues, it will only exacerbate the pending retirement crisis.

Investing is all about the future, not the past. Corporate earnings drive stock prices. The stock market cares about current earnings and anticipated future earnings, not what transpired in the past. The past is the past. Focus on the future.

Investors always face several unknowns: you don't know what will happen in the future and you don't know how the market will react to these future events. In other words, no one can predict the market and do not waste your energy trying. Future rates of return are always unpredictable but aging is guaranteed!

Remember, only about 50% of adults currently invest in the stock market in some form. I want you to join this group of enlightened everyday investors as a way to build your personal wealth for the future. Participating in the financial markets is one of the best ways for everyday investors to achieve financial security over time.

Looking ahead, the fundamentals of the US economy appear to be generally positive. The unemployment rate is low, real wages are gradually improving, consumer spending has begun to rise and inflation has remained low. We have enjoyed a long period of low interest rates, which have helped stimulate borrowing demand for everything from home refinance, to new home purchases, to autos to corporate bond offerings. While the Federal Reserve Bank has signaled they plan to gradually raise interest rates over time, interest rates remain below the level where, historically, they may have caused the economy to slow down or shrink.

I believe everyday investors can achieve success in building wealth for the future by committing to a path, as outlined in this book, that is more binary. That path should include two preferred personal attributes such as developing financial wellness on a regular basis and investing with purpose. Without these two desirable traits, everyday investors are at risk of being lost in the financial wilderness without a compass.

I remain optimistic about the future and believe that stock market returns will be compelling across the broad spectrum of the total stock market over the coming years. I believe investing in the stock market is one of the few options available to stay ahead of inflation. The future purchasing power of your retirement accounts will depend on it. These positive attributes of the economy today should encourage individuals to invest now for the future.

Investing Allows You to Take Charge of Your Future

Invest with Purpose

Compound Interest is Your Friend

Close the Longevity Gap

Take Charge of Your Future

4

CHOICES

If you like brain teasers or solving riddles, here is one for you. What does eating out versus taking your lunch to work, buying one or two cups of coffee daily, earning just 1% less on savings or investment accounts and being a member of the "gig economy" all have in common? Give up? Each of these can have a major, negative impact on your financial future. I will show you why in the remainder of this book.

Remember when your mother told you to be careful about the friends you make, to always eat breakfast, as it was the most important meal of the day, or to put on clean clothes each morning as you headed off to work or school? As it turned out, she was right on all three counts. She was enabling you early on in making good daily choices about how you lived your young life.

Now that you are an adult, unless you still carry your mother's voice around in your head, you create your own future through the daily choices you make. These choices directly impact your ability to save and/or to forego the instant gratification of something today for something more valuable tomorrow like longer-term financial security.

Here is the Merriam-Webster dictionary definition of choices:

- The act of choosing, as in selection
- The power of choosing, as in option
- Care in selecting

The word choice suggests the opportunity or option of choosing freely. The point of this book is to help you make better choices when it comes to your retirement planning.

Start with taking personal responsibility for the decisions you make. This is part of being an adult. Do not blame anyone else for the choices you make, as this is your life. Look in the mirror each morning and make a commitment to yourself to make this a productive day and to perform your daily tasks at the best of your ability. It all starts with a positive attitude! After all, attitudes can be contagious.

The initial question asked in many presentations on investing and retirement planning is "How do I save?" To save is to set aside funds. To invest is to spend money with the expectation of achieving a profit. There is a difference!

Every adult knows they should save for the future but so many fail to do so. Why? I think it is a matter of the lack of financial discipline. When you develop a purpose or plan for saving and you stick with it over time, I call this financial discipline. You may also call it your personal behavior or self-discipline.

Life is all about choices and the choices we make every day help shape the present as well as our future. A few examples of the types of choices people make when it comes to saving and investing or choosing to live paycheck to paycheck include:

- Type of car your drive: new model or functional, older model; top of the line model or one of the middle of the price range models
- Hours you work vs. hours you play daily: is one more time consuming than the other
- Whether you are a spender or a saver: always save something or suffer too much month left at the end of the money
- Do you buy soda to drink or can you be satisfied with water
- Do you waste money on cigarettes or only buy the groceries you need
- Do you pay your required child support or choose to ignore this responsibility and instead go on weekend parties or binges

- Do you take your lunch to work, cook meals at home or eat out often
- Do you buy Starbucks or McDonalds coffee everyday: why not brew it at home
- Do you live below your earnings level or do you spend everything you make
- Do you set goals with a plan for accomplishment or just wander through life aimlessly without any plans

This is not an all-inclusive list of the examples of choices we each make on a daily basis. Rather, it is intended to illustrate the many ways we can approach our lives, differently. By thinking and acting with some regard for the future, potential consequences or with new perspectives, we can dramatically change the outcomes by our decisions. I call it tweaking your daily routine.

My role is not to replace your mother with my opinions and advice about how you should live your life or what you should do or not do in any given situation. I offer these ideas to stimulate your thinking about what is important and not so important to you, no one else. As long as you have good health and stay alive, the future will happen. Why not shape it into the type of future you want with some planning and execution today?

Americans seem to have too many issues when it comes to financial literacy. I am not sure why but I think it may have to do with the lack of adequate financial emphasis in our educational system at both the high school and college levels. I think a robust defense of the status quo is the biggest impediment to making changes in our educational curriculum. For example, if we did not teach financial wellness last year, why should we add it this year? If we add a course on financial wellness, what course are we willing to give up in replacement? It is easier to just keep doing the same thing, year after year, and make no changes.

If individuals are going to be responsible for planning their own retirement, we, as a nation, need to challenge and enhance the educational curriculum to give everyday investors the proper tools to be successful with this all-important task.

A lack of financial literacy is only one component of the problem. The other, which is directly related, is your personal financial behavior. As individuals gain financial literacy, they need to apply that knowledge to their financial behavior. Saving and investing with purpose is the new behavior desired. This is the beginning step to address and help solve a looming future retirement crisis. If you do not change your behavior, nothing will change with your financial future.

One example of applying new facts learned as part of a course on financial literacy to change your personal financial behavior is understanding the Rule of 72. This simple financial formula is used to estimate the length of time in years required to double an investment or account balance at a fixed, annual rate of interest. It is a good illustration of how compound interest works in the real world. Here is how this guideline works:

Rule of 72

$$\frac{72}{5.0\%} = 14.4 \text{ years for any amount to double in value } 5.0\%$$

The above example shows that an investment earning 5.0% per annum will double in 14.4 years. This formula is excellent in highlighting the importance of starting to save early and often. It does not matter what the amount of the initial balance may be. However, the larger the initial investment balance the larger that account will grow over time.

Table of Returns versus Doubling

Interest Rate	Years to Double/Rule of 72
1%	72
3%	24
5%	14
7%	10.3
9%	8
10%	7.2

The table above illustrates the importance of earning just a little more on a bank account or investment. With just a small increase in rate the number of years to double reduces dramatically. Notice the difference in years between earning 3% or 5%?

The power of compound interest really kicks in the longer money is invested. Assume you are 25 years of age and have saved $10,000 in a retirement account. If the account is earning 7.2% per year, the money should double every 10 years (72 divided by 7.2% = 10 years). Here is how that translates into substantial retirement balances at full retirement age (FRA) of sixty-seven.

Age	Account Value
25	$10,000
35	20,000
45	40,000
55	80,000
65	160,000
67 (FRA)	183,800

"Compound interest is the greatest mathematical discovery of all time."

Albert Einstein

These numbers in the table above assume no additional funds are added or invested over these 42 years. Most people will add funds over time to their retirement accounts. These numbers also do not reflect the negative impact of any fees, taxes or the impact of inflation.

Time can be your best friend or worst enemy. It is up to you if you want time to be on your side or working against you. This is yet another choice! The Rule of 72 only works when you have put invested funds to work. Saving money in a mason jar will not grow!

My father always told me "It is ok to spend money, just do not waste it. Earning money is hard work for which you deserve some benefit." I do not want you to think I am against spending money on things you want or need. That is not the point. I want you to think before you spend on what are the benefits you may derive from current spending compared to the benefits of investing. The last thing I want is for you to believe that spending is some type of vice and that investing is the ultimate virtue. I just want you to make better spending decisions, having considered the near and long-term potential consequences of your expenditures. My hope is you will stop robbing the future just because you want a new iphone today.

Some financial professionals earn their living by making the investment process complicated. In this way they justify selling products or creating investment plans they say will help you navigate through the maze of investing to become a successful investor. Much of this advice is very valuable for some, more accredited investors seeking to take advantage of special market conditions or anomalies between markets. Sometimes they promote the advantages of specialized products involving shorting stocks, using puts and calls in the option market, the use of margin in leveraging the returns from investing or other esoteric investment products.

For most of us, as everyday investors, we do not need this more advanced, technical approach to investing to be successful. If you are truly committed to being a long-term investor and you like to do-it-yourself while still having time to enjoy life, there are easier solutions to solving the investment process. This is what this book is about.

Life does not have to be complicated unless we make it that way. For example, there are only seven (7) primary colors: red, orange, yellow, green, blue, indigo and violet. Look at what Michelangelo produced with those colors! In music there are only seven (7) primary notes in an octave and yet listen to what Beethoven created! There are only ten (10) numbers in our numerical system using base 10: zero-nine. Look in amazement at the mathematical formulas and algorithms we have been able to develop from such a small base! No, life does not need to be complicated, so why do we make it that way?

According to the legendary and highly successful football coach, Lou Holtz,[5] there are only four (4) things you need in life:

- Something to do – like a job or career
- Someone to love – like a spouse, family and pets
- Something to believe in – like Christianity or Judaism or some higher being
- Something to hope for – like a comfortable retirement, a long life or a better life for your children

There is a basic rule of nature that says, "You are either growing or dying." This is true for a tree or flowers, for a marriage or for a career. Your individual responsibility is to do the best you can do every day at whatever the task. Not

---

[5] The 3 Rules to a Less Complicated Life, by Lou Holtz, www.youtube.com

everyone will be selected for the starting team or win the award ribbons, but everyone can be the best at whatever you are capable of being. Work toward achieving and fulfilling your personal potential. A friend of mine is fond of saying "There is no heavier burden than unfulfilled potential." You are capable, though, of doing the required heavy lifting to achieve your potential.

Do not complicate your life. Do not over think the need for saving and investing. If you develop financial discipline, it will become a habit to live below your means and save some amount of money from whatever you earn. The decision to begin investing is your choice. Once you make that choice, invest following the guidelines outlined in this book and you will be on your way to building wealth for the future.

Along this path, you will need to maintain a steady course of investing without regard to short-term changes in the market value of your portfolios. Most of us do not worry about the long-term value of our home, nor do we fret about the future value of our automobile. Yet, these are two of the most expensive assets many of us own. We do not worry about these ultimate values because they seem far off in the future and the future values are beyond our control. We need to adopt the same approach to how we look at our investment portfolios. Losing sleep over the future value of any investment portfolio is a loser's game, with nothing to be gained other than a headache or stomach ulcers.

EVERY INVESTOR NEEDS TO BE REMINDED THAT DAILY DECISIONS HAVE AN INFLUENCE ON YOUR FUTURE FINANCIAL WELL BEING

Self Motivation	Potential Consequences
Wander from day to day without a plan for self improvement	Living paycheck to paycheck without any measurable savings
Make some plans but keep them short term in nature	Initially build some savings but because your plans are short term, no lasting benefits for your long-term financial security
Big goals for the future of a long-term nature, like retirement funding	May require living below your means while you seek longer-term benefits. Requires financial discipline.

The choices you make throughout your life define your priorities. Making choices that keep investing for future wealth building opportunities, as a priority, is a wise decision. You and your family will enjoy the benefits.

Ultimately, the choices you make need to translate into doing or taking positive action. You have to use opportunity when it is available, not ignore it or wait for a better deal to come along.

Lifestyle choices, wrote the sociologist Anthony Giddens, are decisions "not only about how to act but who to be." What kind of future and who do you want to become in that future are all wrapped together. This is the real do-it-yourself project of living today while planning for a bright and fulfilling future in retirement.

This is all the background you need to move on to the fundamentals of successful investing. The journey is part of the process; the result of your investment decisions will be your common destination.

There is a Trade-Off Between Choices

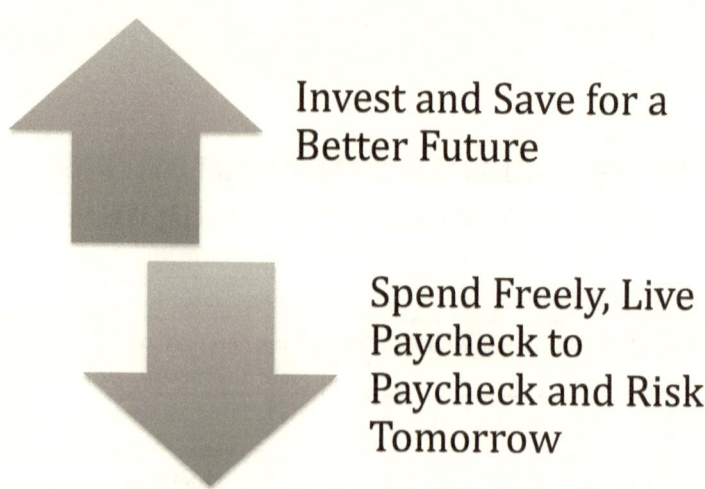

Invest and Save for a Better Future

Spend Freely, Live Paycheck to Paycheck and Risk Tomorrow

PART II

FUNDAMENTALS

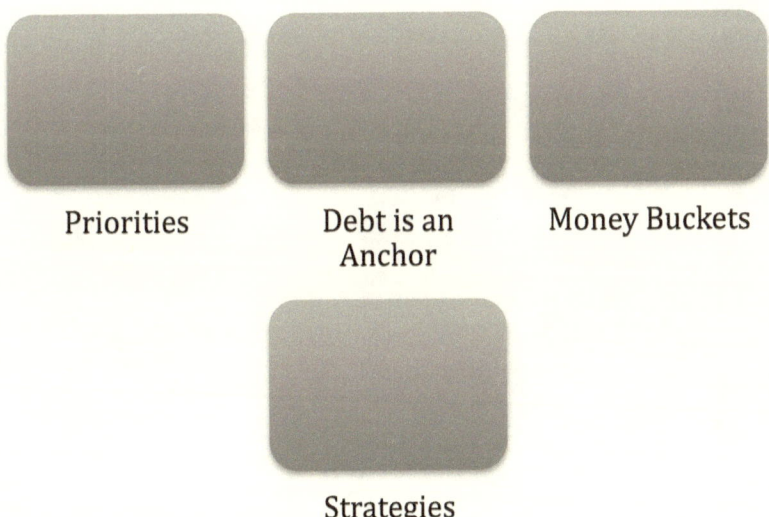

Priorities   Debt is an Anchor   Money Buckets

Strategies

5

CHAPTER

PRIORITIES

Don't major in minors! Avoid the trivial pursuit of the unimportant.

Focus on the BIG picture and concentrate on dealing with those things you can control. Major decisions require your attention and priority. The little things in life will take care of themselves.

When setting priorities, do not start at the bottom of your list with the most minor projects. Purpose could be substituted for priority here. Always tackle your priorities from the most difficult first. Once you set your priorities, live your priorities by incorporating them in your everyday routine.

In my experience there are seven (7) requirements for your financial wellness that, when completed and funded, offer you and your family basic financial protection. I call these my major priorities. These seven (7) should be met and funded **before** you begin to invest. The only exceptions are investing in tax-sheltered investments like a Roth IRA, traditional IRAs or company-sponsored 401(k) plans. Both the IRA and 401(k) plan should be funded as soon as possible.

Financial Wellness

1. Emergency cash fund
2. Health insurance
3. Disability insurance

4. Life insurance
5. A 401(k) plan or a solo 401(k) plan
6. An Individual Retirement Account (IRA), either a traditional IRA or Roth IRA
7. A savings habit

Emergency Cash Fund

This means just what it says. If you do not set aside funds to cover future emergencies, who will? Think of this as one type of rainy day fund. I believe so strongly in having an emergency cash fund that I have dedicated additional discussion on this subject. See Chapter 7 for a more detailed explanation of this concept.

Health Insurance

One of your most important obligations is to take care of your personal health and the healthcare needs of your family. Sign up for the healthcare plan where you work. This medical coverage will usually be the least cost option for healthcare, as you are part of a group plan spreading the risks of healthcare over a larger pool of employees. Be sure to include coverage for both yourself as well as your family.

If you are self-employed, you still need health insurance. You can buy medical coverage on the private market or access health insurance through one of the state sponsored health exchanges under the Affordable Care Act. No one can afford to be without healthcare coverage. Make this a priority. If you are single, this is still one of the most important things you can do for yourself and for those who love you.

A quick note about long-term care insurance. This is the insurance to help cover nursing home and some in-home healthcare needs later in life. I used to recommend people age 65 or older should consider buying this type of coverage as an asset protection measure. I no longer make this recommendation. The long-term care insurance market has shrunk over the years as insurance companies grossly underestimated the costs and length of stay for these future services. Many of them have either withdrawn from this market or increased the premiums to the point the coverage is too expensive. I now recommend healthy retirees should consider a form of self-insurance for these potential expenses. Do not ignore these potential future costs but, rather, plan on being able to cover up to $250,000 of nursing home expenses for one or both spouses. This form of self-insurance will give you peace of mind.

Disability Insurance

Your ability to work and earn a living is one of your most important physical abilities. Do not risk losing this ability through an accident or serious health issue.

Disability insurance is reasonably priced and will give you peace of mind and a monthly check in the event you become disabled. This is insurance you need whether single or married.

There is a maximum dollar limit on how much disability insurance you can purchase. Insurance companies limit the dollar amount of disability coverage as a way to discourage fraudulent claims. Most companies will limit the dollar amount of disability coverage to 60% of your current earned income. There are a few exceptions for higher limits for specific professions who may need a higher threshold for coverage. Talk with an insurance agent.

Life Insurance

I am not an insurance salesman but I recognize the value and importance of having life insurance coverage. Life insurance is intended to offer financial benefits to your beneficiaries in the event of your untimely death or upon your death after living to a ripe old age. If you are single, I recommend you consider term insurance. This is usually cheaper and covers a specific period of time. You might want to consider a 20-year term policy in an amount to at least cover your burial expenses and a little left over for your designated beneficiaries.

If married with a family to support, I recommend a combination of term and whole life insurance. You have more financial responsibilities when you are married and this combination of coverage should give you the satisfaction that you have provided some financial support when you are no longer around.

Term insurance can be for a limited number of years, say while the children are under the age of 18-21 and probably living at home. I recommend you supplement this term coverage with some whole life insurance, sometimes called permanent life insurance. The point in adding whole life insurance is to lock in a fixed premium for the rest of your life. The younger you are and the healthier you are when you first take out whole life insurance will result in the premium being at a lower rate than if the insurance is taken later in life. Whole life also can give you guaranteed coverage for life if you develop some uninsurable condition later. This is an option to add to basic coverage. It just makes good sense to provide life insurance coverage for your family.

You will notice I have avoided recommending any dollar amount of either disability or life insurance coverage. All insurance is a very personal decision. Your personal circumstances, age, current health condition and life style may all impact the cost of insurance. Also, there are many insurance options available as add-ons to basic insurance coverage. These are all subject to your decisions and not in the purview of this book.

Participate in a 401(k) Plan

Many employers offer their employees a 401(k) plan that is a tax advantaged investment plan for retirement. This and healthcare coverage are two of the most popular employee benefits. Enrollment usually requires a minimum time of service with the employer unless you work for a company that does automatic enrollment of all employees into their 401(k) plan as soon as they join the company.

The investment options in a 401(k) plan may not be ideal, but the tax advantages of the plan can make up for any deficit in these options.

Many companies that offer a 401(k) plan also offer a matching program. It is not uncommon for the company match to equal 3-5 percent or more of an employee's gross salary as a match. This means the company will add 3-5% of the employee's salary to your 401(k) account IF the employee has contributed an equal or greater amount during the year. For example, if you have an annual salary of $50,000, the company may add $1500.00 (3%) to your 401(k) account, usually at yearend, as a match. This is free money and is well worth the monthly deduction from your salary to fund your portion of the contribution. To contribute 3% of your salary, the monthly contribution would be $125.00 in this example. Do not pass up these matching programs. Always find a way to contribute an amount equal to the company match, as a minimum.

If you must make a choice between funding a 401(k) account that includes a company match or an Individual Retirement Account (IRA), always fund the 401(k) account first. It is important to take advantage of the company match. I hope you will find a way to fund both.

Vesting is another question that often comes up in Q&A sessions on 401(k) plans. Most 401(k) plans that offer a matching component have a vesting schedule. Many times this is 3-5 years of on-going participation in the plan as a requirement to receive or own 100% of the company match. Call this one form of a golden handcuff to keep you contributing to the plan and to maintain your employment with the same employer over the term of the vesting schedule.

For example, if the company plan has a 5-year vesting schedule, this usually means you earn 20% of the annual company match each year. After 5 years, the entire company match belongs to you. If you leave that employer after you are fully vested in their 401(k) plan, the entire amount of your account can be transferred in a tax-free IRA rollover. Always read the fine print about vesting requirements in any 401(k) plan in which you participate.

In 2018 the maximum individual contribution limit for 401(k) plans has been increased to $18,500.00, while the catch-up provision for employees age 50 or older is $6,000.00. This means if you contribute at the maximum level and you are age 50 or older, you can put away $24,500.00 a year. This is a significant amount that can grow tax-advantaged until you retire and begin to withdraw from the account or complete an IRA rollover. Always check with the web site irs.gov for the most current limitations

If you are self-employed, there is an alternative 401(k) product for you. This is the solo 401(k) or self-directed 401(k) plan. This self-employed 401(k) is a qualified retirement plan that works along the same guidelines as a company sponsored plan EXCEPT the contribution limits are higher.

- A total of up to $55,000.00 can be contributed annually to a solo 401(k) in 2018, with an additional $6,000.00 catch-up contribution, if age 50 or older
- Contrast the solo 401(k) with a company sponsored 401(k) plan contribution limits of $18,500.00 in 2018 with a $6,000.00 catch-up contribution for ages 50 or older
- Both plans offer the same pre-tax deduction from your salary and the earnings are tax deferred until you begin to withdraw funds in retirement
- It is possible to participate in both a solo 401(k) and a company sponsored 401(k) at the same time, if you meet the requirements

If you work for a company offering a pension plan, thrift or stock purchase plan or other types of benefits, I encourage you to participate in them, if available. All of these types of benefits should improve your retirement planning results.

Fund an Individual Retirement Account (IRA)

The most basic building block of retirement planning is the Individual Retirement Account (IRA). 2018 individual contribution limits remain unchanged at $5,500.00 with a catch-up limit for people age 50 or older of $1,000.00. Being able to invest up to $6,500.00 annually in a tax-advantaged IRA is another powerful wealth builder.

I believe every individual should invest in an IRA as soon as they become eligible. To contribute to an IRA, the basic requirement is earned income. There is one exception for nonworking spouses, called a spousal IRA. Provided one spouse has wages or self-employment income, contributions can be made to a separate spousal IRA. The limits for each IRA are the same. The sooner you begin funding an IRA, the longer it will have to grow on a compound basis. I like the provisions for a Roth IRA, versus a traditional IRA, particularly for younger investors. Either can become the foundation of your retirement plan. See income limitations to qualify for a Roth IRA in the table below.

Roth and Traditional IRA Comparisons

Roth IRA 2018	Contribution limits are $5,500 plus $1,000 for age 50+ and are after tax. Withdrawals at any time are tax-free. There is a maximum income threshold limit of $135,000 if single and $199,000 if filing jointly. There are no required minimum distributions after FRA.
Traditional IRA 2018	Contribution limits of $5,500 plus $1,000 for age 50+ are pre-tax. Withdrawals after full retirement age (FRA) are taxable as ordinary income. Contributions may be tax deductible, subject to limitations. After age 70½, required minimum distributions (RMD) must be taken or be subject to a penalty.

Source: Internal Revenue Service[6]

---

[6] Individual Retirement Account Contribution Limits, www.irs.gov

The Internal Revenue Service sets the annual contribution limits for both traditional IRAs and Roth IRAs. The limits for both in 2018 are unchanged with $5,500 plus $1,000 catch up for age 50 and older.

With a traditional IRA, contributions are often tax deductible. This is one of the biggest advantages of the traditional IRA over the Roth IRA. Roth IRAs are funded with after tax contributions and are *never* tax deductable.

The tax deduction for traditional IRAs is *before ADJUSTED GROSS INCOME (AGI)*. This can be a very valuable deduction as Federal taxes are calculated on the AGI number. The lower the AGI, the less tax to be paid.

Tax deductibility for a traditional IRA is subject to these three (3) rules:

1. If you *are* eligible for a retirement plan at work (including 401(k) plans), your ability to take a deduction is limited to lower income levels.

    - Single $63,000 – 73,000
    - Married, filing joint   101,000 – 121,000

If your AGI is less than $63,000, you qualify for a full deduction. If your AGI is above $73,000, then no deduction is allowed. If your AGI falls between these numbers, then you are allowed a partial deduction. It works the same way for the married, filing joint tax return.

2. If you are *not* eligible to participate in a retirement plan at work, your tax deductibility for contributions is *not* limited, unless your spouse is covered at her place of work. In this case, combined AGI of $189,000 or less can take a full deduction.
3. Even if you cannot take any deductions for your traditional IRA contributions, they are still very worthwhile. They provide a tax-deferred investment account to build upon for your future retirement.

Contributions to both types of IRAs can be made until April 15th of the year following a specific tax year. For example, for tax year 2018, you have 15 ½ months to fund an IRA (January 1, 2018 – April 15, 2019). This allows you to make a monthly contribution of $368/month (for $5,500 maximum) or $434/month (for $6,500 maximum).

Establish a Savings Habit

As stated earlier in Chapter 3, savings is the first requirement to have funds available for investing. Many financial advisors recommend individuals should save 15 percent or more of their gross salary annually. By definition then, living below your earnings level is a requirement to generate funds for savings. Accept the fact this is the only way you begin to set aside funds for investing for your future financial security.

In a recent Wall Street Journal article, the difficulty everyday investors have with establishing a savings habit was highlighted. According to that article, the personal savings rate in the USA has dropped to a 10 year low. As of the end of December 2017, the personal savings rate had fallen to 2.4%. This is the percentage of savings of gross income for the average American. This is far below the 15% of gross income needed to achieve investment success for retirement and other long-term goals. With a savings rate this low, it could be one sign of a potential, growing risk of underfunded retirement accounts.

You need to overcome this resistance to savings by setting aside 10-15% of your gross income each month. Savings deposited into a money market account or a bank savings account is a start. Automate this process by setting up a payroll deduction or automatic bank transfer of funds directly from your payroll account to a savings account. Periodically, withdraw funds from the savings account to begin investing as outlined earlier in this chapter. If you can sustain this savings procedure for at least six (6) months, it will become a savings habit.

Having put in place these seven (7) must have protections for you and your family, you are now ready to begin the next phase of the investing process. Successful investing always starts with a plan. I like to put a plan in writing so I will not vary from the original goal. This plan should highlight your priorities for putting aside funds and investing with purpose. It is ok to have more than one purpose for investing. As you achieve the first priority you can move on to the second and so forth. Personally, I think you should establish and fund the retirement accounts first, keeping them active while you work on shorter term goals like saving for a car or a down payment on a house.

Examples of priorities for saving and investing might include:

- Down payment on a house
- Purchase a newer car or truck
- Building a 529 plan to finance college expenses for each child
- Building a financially secure retirement

These and other personal priorities give you focus on why you are investing and create a tangible, measureable goal. Once you have set a goal, the goal should be refined to include the dollar amount needed to achieve the goal. When you have reached this amount in your investment accounts, you know you have been successful in meeting that priority. A sense of accomplishment can be a powerful self-motivator!

A common theme from some of my discussions with people in the millennial generation is their focus on near term goals while exclusively avoiding longer-term goals. Money for a new car or saving for a down payment on a house is two examples of these near term goals. I applaud the near term goals but also, I advise on the importance of including longer-term goals, like saving for retirement. By definition, longer-term goals will take a longer time period to achieve success. By not including them in their purpose for investing, they are unwittingly exacerbating the achievement of the longer-term goal.

Getting Started

Here are five (5) steps to launch your personal goal of investing with purpose:

1. Set a goal; what is the total dollar amount required to successfully achieve the goal?
2. Determine your time frame: months, years, decades
3. Remain in control and commit your plan to writing
4. Develop financial discipline
5. Make adjustments along the way

See one example of how to implement these steps at the end of this chapter.

Setting a goal with a specific dollar amount as a target creates a definition for success. In this way you can measure your progress toward achieving your goal. It will tell you if you are on track or if you need to increase your savings rate to be successful.

Determine your time frame means establishing how many months or years you expect to be investing to achieve the goal. For example, to save and invest for a down payment on a house might take longer than saving for a newer car. The time frame chosen will help you decide how much and how often to save and invest.

Remain in control simply means to never take your eye off the purpose for investing. There will always be obstacles thrown in your way to continue to invest or alternatives for spending money this month or next that takes you off course from meeting your investment goals. You must remain in charge and stay focused on why you are investing. Do not fall prey to straying expenditures that make no contribution toward attaining your goal.

Write out your plan with goals, time frame, and dollar amount of each goal when successfully achieved to help prevent goal creep. We all tend to fudge on our achievements if we get close to the goal or something more interesting comes along.

If you do not have a written plan, you have nothing more than a wing and a prayer for the future.

Developing financial discipline is a lifelong endeavor. Financial discipline means putting aside an amount of money consistently and investing it in accordance with your plan. It is like an exercise routine. If you do it long enough, it will become habit. Stray from your routine and the expected benefits from the exercise will be as elusive as the Yeti.

Making adjustments along the way is the smart way to respond to changes in the economy, your lifestyle or the state of your family. Life happens and things change, no matter how much you want them to stay the same. Be flexible and make small adjustments, as needed. Do not make wholesale changes in your investment plan unless you have no other choices.

Components of Success

Components	Comments
Time in the market and the power of compound interest working for you	Stay fully invested and avoid jumping in and out of the market. The enemy of the success of this component is moving in and out of the market. This is called market timing.
Patience and persistence	Financial discipline is a work in progress not just the outcome of one or two intentional behaviors. Stay the course and stay focused on the long-term goal, not periodic fluctuations in valuations.
Need for discretionary income	Always set aside some funds for spending on entertainment and other nonessential purchases
Set a goal for each specific purpose	Do not let the journey become the destination; have a purpose to your financial wealth building
Automate the process	Never miss a transfer to your intended money bucket; put it on auto-pilot
Achieve Financial Wellness	The first stage of success resulting from implementing the 5 step process of investing with purpose
Transition from an asset accumulator to an efficient income drawdown strategy after you enter retirement	Live the dream you have always had about retirement. Manage the withdrawal rate from your retirement funds.

EXAMPLE OF GOAL SETTING

STEPS	DEFINE THE GOAL	EXPECTED RESULTS
State the Goal	To fund retirement accounts to achieve at least a $1,000,000 balance at age 67 (FRA)	$1,142,000
Time Frame	32 years	Assumes starting at age 35 and FRA is 67
Anticipated Annual Return	5.0%	Below the historical return for the stock market
Fully fund IRA annually	$5,500 x 32 years @ 5.0% return by investing $460 each month	$424,314
Fund 401(k) annually	Assume funding at 50% of maximum or $9250 per year x 32 years @ 5.0% by investing $775 each month	$717,742
Develop Financial Discipline	Fund both IRA and 401(k) accounts monthly	Automate the investments to fund monthly through payroll deductions or auto transfers
Make adjustments	None needed	Goal Achieved

CHAPTER

6

DEBT ANCHOR

This is a no-brainer. Get out of debt! You have heard similar advice from your parents and grandparents. So why do so many people enter retirement with more debt than they have in savings? This would be a disaster!

Financial discipline is a process, not just the outcome of occasional intentional behaviors. Financial discipline also implies staying with your commitment to fund your investment accounts with regularity. Wealth building for the future absolutely requires financial discipline.

Debt has been both revered and reviled by financial analysts and some Wall Street professionals. Debt is an anchor, holding you back and dragging you further behind in the wealth building process. Debt is an impediment to your ability to free up cash for investments and discretionary spending. Yet some investing professionals promote the advantages of debt as leverage to increase the return on some investments. Do not be lulled into using debt in any form for your investment accounts.

Stockbrokers and money managers talk in terms of margin debt as a way to grow your portfolio beyond an all cash approach to buying stocks. Stay with the more conservative approach of operating on an all cash basis. Margin debt may work for investment professionals but I do not recommend taking on debt for any investment purposes for everyday investors.

Debt comes in many shapes, sizes and with various demands. All debt should be repaid as soon as practical. Here are some of the most common categories of individual debt:

- Credit cards – You cannot carry a balance on a credit card month-to-month and build wealth at the same time. These concepts are an oxymoron, to say the least. Credit cards may have some of the highest interest rates of all categories of debt. Always payoff credit card debt in a sequence from the highest interest rate to the lowest. Once repaid, pay off the credit card balance monthly. If you can't, stop using a credit card, cut it up and only use cash. Interest paid on credit card debt is not tax deductible.
- Student loans-Address them; don't hide from them; pay them off. These loans are how you were able to afford college. They deserve your attention.

Interest may be partially deductible. Make it a priority to pay these off on schedule. No one owes you a free ride.

- Auto loans – Pay as you go; reduce faster with accelerated payments. Interest on auto loans is not tax deductible. Pay off the auto loans on schedule and, if you have extra money, apply additional payments to reduce the balance faster.
- Mortgage Loans – Interest paid is tax-deductible. This is the last debt to repay. Start with a 30-year, fixed rate mortgage to have the lowest monthly payment. As you payoff other debt, increase your mortgage payments.

Eventually, refinance into a 15-year, fixed rate mortgage. This will save you a substantial amount of money over the life of the loan by reducing the total amount of interest paid. As long as you qualify to deduct the interest on a home mortgage, this can be called "good debt."

- Home Equity Line of Credit (HELOC) – This is a revolving line of credit that taps into the equity in your home. This is a second mortgage on your residence. Usually, there are no fees for nonuse. In 2018 interest may be deductible on the HELOC, if the funds are used to make improvements on the residence and the taxpayer meets all other requirements. Check with your tax preparer for clarification.

- Other debt (like department store credit, miscellaneous cash advances or any other type of consumer debt) – always payoff the highest interest rate first and work progressively to the lowest rate. It is really this simple. Once out of debt, stay out of debt

The order in which you repay debt can make a difference on your reported taxable income. Pay off non-tax deductible debt first[7], preserving tax-deductible debt as the last to be repaid. Here is the order in which I would repay personal debt based on the current tax deductibility of the interest as of December 2017:

- Credit card debt
- Auto loans
- Student loan debt
- Any other consumer debt
- Home Equity Line of Credit
- Mortgage loan

Timely debt repayment is always important because it will affect your overall credit rating. The credit reporting companies like Equifax, TransUnion and Experian will report to any requesting merchant a summary of your credit history and calculate a credit score (known as a FICO score) based on your past reported payment history. The higher the credit score, the lower your credit risks. These scores range from 300-850 as follows:

FICO SCORECARD[8]

- 800 + = Exceptionally good credit (850 is the maximum score)
- 740-799 = Very good credit
- 670-739 = Good credit score
- 580-669 = Fair credit score
- Below 579 = Poor credit score

---

[7] Tax Deductible Publication 17, Your Federal Income Tax for Individuals and Publication 550, Investment Interest and Expenses; www.irs.gov

[8] FICO Score, www.investopedia.com

With a high credit score, you will receive the lowest interest rate and the best repayment terms on future financing requests. The opposite is also true. Credit scores of 600 or less usually pay the highest interest rates or run the risk of having their request for credit being denied. Keeping all debt repayment current and on schedule can help you keep more money in your pocket on future purchases through reduced borrowing costs.

Wealth building does not happen when you are burdened with debt. Paying off debt as quickly as is reasonable and then staying out of debt is a good habit to adopt. Your investing capacity will be greatly enhanced.

A recent Prudential 2017 study found that 6 out of 10 workers are stressed about their current financial situation. This is a shocking indicator of the need for the availability of more financial literacy and financial wellness resources and tools to help people manage their financial lives. Some workers have become trapped in a debt cycle that must be broken.

Job training requirements and the pace of work are changing faster than ever as innovation and structural changes are transforming work faster than our institutions and individuals can adapt. Full time equivalents (FTE) are shrinking in numbers employed while "gig economy" workers are growing in the workforce.

These are daunting challenges where financial opportunities come and go at increasing speeds. You must find a way to take advantage of these new opportunities when they are available.

Trying to stay competitive in a rapidly changing economy requires skill, knowledge, flexibility and personal accountability. It requires agility to stay ahead and to get ahead. Carrying a burden of debt only slows you down. Servicing debt is like running a race with one arm tied behind your back and both legs bound together (remember the potato sack race). Find a way to get out of debt and stay out of debt so you can increase your economic opportunities through investing.

Debt is a heavy burden and an anchor! It does more damage to your wealth building activities than just holding you still in the water. The lead weight of too much debt pulls more people underwater than it helps others to achieve their stated purpose for investing. The debt anchor actually moves you further behind in the process of building a secure financial future through effective wealth building. Do not let debt drown your hopes for the future.

7

MONEY BUCKETS

Before I discuss the importance of creating an emergency cash fund, known as a rainy day fund, let me spend some time introducing the concept of four separate "money buckets" when it comes to allocating funds for living.

Finding a way to segregate funds intended for different purposes has always been a challenge for many people. I have a friend who does this process mentally while maintaining all his funds co-mingled in one account. I think he is the exception. For most of us, we need a more graphically simple way to separate funds. The visual metaphor that works for me is the following categories I use for physically segregating funds:

Money Buckets

- Emergency funds
- Living Expenses
- Discretionary funds
- Investment funds

I call these categories my "money buckets" because this term gives me a clear, mental image of buckets filling with cash where each bucket is ear marked for specific purposes. This concept has worked for me and I believe, if you try it, it will work for you.

Emergency Funds –Money Bucket #1

This is a continuation of the explanation I started in Chapter 5. Each of us should have learned from experience how often unexpected expenses pop up. They always do and you should anticipate the need to address them. Being able to fund these surprise expenditures without creating financial stress is an important part of maturity. Call it planning for the unexpected or anticipating future expenses not yet incurred.

Most financial advisors suggest putting aside funds for these unplanned and unanticipated expenses (again, call it a rainy day fund). Anywhere between three to six (3-6) months of living expenses is the recommended dollar amount. These funds should be kept separate from all other funds. They should be held in an account that has liquidity, such as a bank account or money market account. The idea is you need to have ready access whenever you need the money without having to sell an investment or other asset at an inopportune time to fund the expense. Seems like good advice.

If the 3-6 months of expenses seems too high of a dollar amount, start with something smaller and increase it over time. As you draw down these rainy day funds from time to time, you will need to replenish them. The only time these idle funds seem like a good idea is when you really need them. I sometimes feel the same way about paying insurance premiums. If I have a casualty loss, however, it sure is nice to have the insurance coverage to offset the majority of the unexpected expense causing the insurance claim.

For example, start with building these emergency funds to equal one (1) months gross pay, then continue on to two (2) and three (3) months of gross pay. You may choose to pause at this point to see how this dollar amount held in reserve works for you. Three months of gross pay may be the right number. If not, continue to build this fund over time to a level consistent with your needs. Using gross pay instead of a percentage of living expenses is just one variation for determining the amount of money needed in an emergency reserve bucket.

Living Expenses – Money Bucket #2

If you have lived independently for any period of time, you know how much you spend each week or month. If you do not, you are a candidate for budgeting. It is important to know what it costs you for living expenses and where you spend your money. Money Bucket #2 usually holds the largest amount of money of the four buckets.

Once you have this number in mind, my suggestion is to maintain three months of living expenses set aside in money bucket #2. Remember, I am assuming you are earning a paycheck at least monthly, so you have incoming cash every month. This will help you maintain the balance in this account. Start with a small amount and add to it over time.

Rome was not built in a day and neither will your money buckets be filled with cash in a few months. It will take time and your financial discipline to fill these buckets to the level you have determined gives you breathing room for any emergency and for everyday expenses.

As discussed in the previous chapter, if you are repaying various forms of debt, this money bucket concept will work, as well. Set aside funds in each bucket labeled with the debt to be repaid and use these funds solely for that purpose. As one debt is extinguished, move on to the next debt to be repaid. Eventually, after all debt has been repaid, there are more funds available for living expenses or investment, as you choose.

Discretionary Funds – Money Bucket #3

As part of my belief that there are always things you want to buy that may not necessarily be needed, why not set aside some funds for these expenses. You know they will happen so why not control how much you will spend in this category. I call this my "fun money."

I recommend setting aside up to 10% of your gross salary for discretionary spending. If you know you already spend more than that, either reduce your spending in this category or save a higher percentage of your gross salary for this money bucket #3. These expenses may include things like movies, entertainment, restaurants, ski trips, vacations, video games, date night and other miscellaneous "fun" expenditures.

For example, if your gross salary is $50,000 annually, setting aside 10% for Money Bucket #3 would be a goal of $5,000. Putting aside $200 per month for 25 months will reach this goal (200 x 25 = 5,000). This is the one money bucket that will most likely never be full.

Investment Funds – Money Bucket #4

What you have left after funding money buckets #1, #2 and #3 from your gross monthly salary goes into money bucket #4 for savings and investing. If you want a percentage target for this money bucket, let's back into it this way.

- Money bucket #1 –Emergency Cash – 3-6 months of living expenses (say 20% of gross salary x 50,000 = $10,000 goal)
- Money bucket #2 – Living Expenses – 3 months actual living expenses (say 50% of gross pay x 50,000 = $25,000 goal)
- Money bucket #3 – Discretionary Spending-Your "fun" or play money (say 10% of gross salary x 50,000 = $5,000 goal)
- Money bucket #4 – Save and Future wealth building – (say 15-20% of gross salary x 50,000 = $10,000 goal)

Compare 3-5 Year Funding Schedule

GOAL	3 YEAR	5 YEARS
Money Bucket #1 $10,000	$280/month	$170/ month
Money Bucket $2 $25,000	$695/ month	$420/ month
Money Bucket #3 $5,000	$140/ month	$85/ month
Money Bucket #4 $10,000	$280/ month	$170/ month

Now you understand the concept of money buckets utilized to meet specific expense categories throughout your life. While the purpose of each money bucket may not change, over time the percentages of how much of your gross salary goes into each money bucket probably will change. Once you have reached the goal of three (3) months living expenses set aside for emergency funds, you can increase the investing percentage. Same is true if and when you can lower your living expenses.

Many times I have been asked if there is a priority ranking in funding these money buckets? I don't think so. Funding all four money buckets each month will help you establish the savings habit. It will also help you to live your newfound, changed financial behavior everyday. Once you overcome the initial inertia to get started, funding all four money buckets simultaneously will accelerate your journey toward wealth building for the future. At this point, financial wellness has become another habit.

While liquidity is an important aspect of where you keep funds set aside for emergency, living and discretionary spending, investment funds need not have such high liquidity requirements. Where should savings and investment funds be held?

Until I have saved enough funds to meet the minimum amount required for a specific investment, I use a money market account with a bank or one of the many, on-line investment websites. I like Fidelity Investments, Vanguard or Schwab as a holding area for these funds. Once I have made my initial investment, I transfer investment funds monthly directly into the fund I have chosen. I automate this process by setting up a recurring transfer request with either a bank or as a direct payroll deduction.

Once you automate the monthly transfers for investments, I call this saving on autopilot. It is a concept modeled after the cockpit autopilot used by pilots. It is a system in which computer software controls most of the airplanes detailed movements while in the air. Airplane autopilots have proven to reduce human error resulting in a safer flying experience for the public. The same can be done for saving and investing. The autopilot concept of funding investment accounts means you have accepted financial discipline into your daily life. You will never miss a monthly contribution toward building wealth for the future. In this way you have now achieved auto pilot status on investing going forward.

FOUR PRIMARY MONEY BUCKETS

EMERGENCY
CASH

LIVING
EXPENSES

DISCRETIONARY
FUNDS

INVESTMENT
FUNDS

8

INVESTMENT STRATEGY OVERLOAD

Before I launch into discussing various investment strategies, each of us must first come to terms with understanding our personal risk tolerance for investing. What does risk tolerance mean? Simply put, risk tolerance means how comfortable you are investing your hard earned money in assets that fluctuate in value and where you could have the potential to lose money. Investments can lose money or even become worthless. This is a risk that scares many beginning investors. If the thought of incurring unrealized losses (a paper loss) on any given day, week, month or quarter gives you a queasy stomach, then I would say you have a very low risk tolerance for investing. Realized losses (actual loses) do not occur until some asset is sold and the price reflects a loss from the original purchase price.

On the other hand, if you can adapt to the concept of being a long-term investor, where portfolio values are more important annually or even further in the future, then I say you have a higher-risk tolerance for investing. I cannot make this determination for you. If you truly have a low risk tolerance for investing, you may be more comfortable in putting your money in FDIC insured bank deposit products, US government bonds or perhaps some guaranteed insurance products. The choice is yours. Just remember the old saying, "Risk and reward are related. The higher the risk, the greater the potential reward should be."

Selecting an investment strategy is one of those paradoxical tasks that can be both exacting and boring, requiring times of intense concentration interspersed with high levels of tedium. Defining your purpose is step one. Deciding on what tools (various asset classes) to use to achieve your investment purpose is the second step.

The USA and world economies are very intertwined, complex and subject to limitless surprises and disasters. Disasters can be man-made or naturally occurring. Political disasters resulting from poor governance like corrupt leaders, monarchies or dictatorships gone awry are frequent throughout history around the world.

The stock market can be an overwhelming topic and confusing marketplace in which to purchase and sell stocks or bonds. Stocks and bonds are my tools of choice. Let's start with the eleven primary sectors in the stock market, as represented in the S&P 500 Index (Standard and Poor's 500 Index). Some call these the fundamental or normal asset sectors.

These eleven (11) sectors or asset classes are listed at the end of this chapter along with a table showing the most current five (5) year history of annual returns by sector (from 2013 through 2017). No need to memorize the various asset categories/sectors or their returns. This is a dynamic tool that changes quarterly based on the actual total returns of the various sectors during that quarter.

What this table illustrates clearly is the fluctuating performance numbers for each asset category or sector from year to year. There is no discernable pattern or predictability for the top or bottom performers or those in between year over year. This chart also makes very clear the importance of maintaining diversification within your portfolio.

If you were an investor in any individual stock or bond within these sectors, how would you manage your position and how would you follow all of the rapid-fire developments that affect the performance of these individual investments? Unless you are a professional investor, it is best to leave the ownership of individual stocks or bonds as a style or strategy alone.

There are two primary investment management categories: active and passive. A third category that some say is between these two is called smart beta, also known as strategic beta. Smart beta funds seek to outperform the market by weighting their portfolio holdings based on something other than traditional market capitalization. The individual holdings are selected on the basis of the investors overall strategy such as value, growth or low volatility. I find smart beta as a style to be too objective and, therefore, I stay away from using it. I recommend you focus on choosing between active and passive investment management.

I define active and passive investment management in the table below.

Here is a brief menu of just a few of the investment strategies[9] being marketed today.

I call this "Choice Overload."

Choice Overload

STRATEGY COMPONENTS

Growth	Focus is on capital appreciation; may include companies with above average growth rates;
Value	Focus is on companies that the market seems to undervalue; also known as stocks trading below their intrinsic value;
GARP	Focus is on stocks that combine both growth and value by selecting companies that may be undervalued and have sustainable growth potential
Balanced	A portfolio allocation balancing risk and return; these portfolios may be equally divided between stocks and bonds
Large Cap	Represented by the Russell 1000 index or the S&P 500 index; consists of companies with a market cap of $10 billion or more
Medium Cap	These stocks tend to have a market cap between $2 billion and $10 billion; Represented by the S&P Midcap 400 index
Small Cap	Represented by the Russell 2000 index; comprised of companies with a market cap of between $300 million and $2 billion

---

[9] 10 Long Term Investing Strategies That Work, www.investingmoney.usnews.com

Domestic	Investing in companies that are primarily based in the USA and whose majority of revenues are derived from sales in the USA; represented by the Russell 3000 index
International	Represented by companies whose revenues are generated outside the USA; represented by the FTSE All-World index
Target date funds	Too conservative and fees are too high; attempt to adjust stock/fixed income balance by age of account holder; some call these "one size fits all" funds which means they are good for some but not for all. These are examples of asset allocation strategies.
Index Funds/ETF	Both revered and reviled by financial planners and some Wall Street professionals; an example of passive investing with low fees;
Hedge Funds	Not for ordinary investors; stay away from these high fee, high risk products
Active management	Professional investment manager who attempts to outperform the market; charges fees and may have other costs
Passive management	Follows a chosen market index; goal is to match that market index; have low expense ratios; offers broad diversification
Annuities	These are not investment products; they are insurance contracts; I recommend considering a fixed or immediate annuity upon retirement with a portion of your retirement dollars. There are other alternatives for creating a monthly income stream.

The Sharpe Ratio	Return divided by volatility; the object is to create investment portfolios with the highest ratio; in this way they promise to deliver the biggest return with the lowest volatility
Sector index funds	These target specific market sectors within the S&P 500 index or other market sectors; focus is too narrow like only financial or energy companies;
Style Rotation	A form of market timing; trying to move from value to growth or from large dividend paying stocks to small cap stocks, all at just the right time;
Emerging Markets	A fund or ETF that invests the majority of its assets in markets of a single developing country or group of countries
Fixed Income Only	Focus is on income; a bond only buy and hold strategy looks to maximize income from assumed safe, individual bonds and hold until maturity; there is still a risk element in bond investing

This list is representative of the alphabet soup of various investment strategies. Strategies can be as diverse as growth versus value, to the future direction of interest rates, versus overall valuation of the market, versus growth in gross domestic product (GDP) and inflation. I call this overwhelming variety of different investment strategies the noise in the markets or "Choice Overload." There are too many investment strategies to count. I recommend you avoid the noise and focus on just a few of these.

Unless you are willing to spend the time and energy to research and analyze various companies, their fundamentals and managements, understand their competitive market position, determine any correlation with the overall market, and many other factors involved in picking winning investments, I recommend staying away from individual stocks or bonds.

To be a good stock picker requires that you become totally immersed in the market. Unless you want to become a professional investor, my recommendation is that individual stocks may be outside the scope of everyday investors. It is not a matter of intelligence; it is about having the time to commit to the research and study of individual companies and their management teams. Most people are consumed by the demands of their career, balancing time with family and some limited free time, leaving no time left over to do the heavy lifting of individual stock research.

Not all is lost for everyday investors, however. Everyday investors have one of the richest men to follow as an example or as a mentor. In 2007, billionaire professional investor Warren Buffett made a personal bet of $1,000,000 that an index fund that invests in the S&P 500 Index could achieve a higher average return than a hedge fund that invests in a portfolio of positions in other hedge funds over a 10 year time period. Protégé Partners, an asset manager, who chose five (5) "funds of funds' as their counter bet, undertook the other side of the bet. These "funds of funds" were managed by some of the smartest traders on Wall Street. The bet was set to expire on December 31, 2017.The index fund chosen by Mr. Buffett was the Vanguard 500 Index Fund Admiral shares. Through the 10 years of this bet, the index fund was up 7.1% compounded annually, while the hedge fund was up a dismal 2.2%. Warren Buffett was proven right again on his preferred choice of investments.

Both parties to the bet pledged their stakes in the bet would be donated to a charity of their personal choice. Mr. Buffett designated Girl, Inc. of Omaha, NE as his beneficiary for this bet.

Part of the success of the index fund over the hedge fund is in the difference in expense structure. The Vanguard Admiral Fund expense ratio is 0.05% annually versus the 2.0% annual fee plus a 20.0% share of profits typical of a hedge fund. Lower investment expenses always make a positive difference in overall returns.

On a more personal note, Mr. Buffett has shared publicly his advice to the trustee of his future estate upon his death. He has instructed the trustee to invest on behalf of his wife and future widow, Astrid Menks, that she will be best served by investing his estate in index funds, upon his death. His reasoning is simple. Index funds let smaller investors share in the gains of the US economy over time, as large, US companies dominant the index. Index funds also allow investors to escape the higher costs of investing with their low expense ratios. He also believes that by investing in this way, most everyday investors can avoid individual companies who might choose less-competent management, run into unforeseen obstacles in the future or who pursue business strategies with high risks.

In his 2014 letter to the shareholders of Berkshire Hathaway, Mr. Buffett very specifically recommended his estates' trustee should invest 90% of his future estate in stock index funds and 10% in short-term US government bonds. His recommendation again mentions using The Vanguard Group of index funds.

I like to think in terms of learning from a successful investors experience and market performance. Warren Buffett has had some outstanding performance years and some years his returns have been below the average for the market. He has been consistent in his investment approach, which is a commitment to long-term, value investing. My conclusion from studying his performance record is that he has found a way to systematize the investment process, without the influence of his personal emotions. This is the take away I want you to gather going forward. For everyday investors finding a way to systematize their investment process can lead to successful wealth building over time. Eliminate emotional decision making, as best you can.

Let's pause a few minutes and go back to square one to define the four basic terms I used in investing.

- Common Stock/Equities
- Bonds
- Index Funds
- Exchange Traded Funds (ETFs)

Common Stock/Equities

These are securities that represent fractional ownership in a publicly traded corporation. Most stocks have voting rights and shareholders are entitled to vote on the election of the board of directors and general corporate policies. Stock is sometimes called shares. The shares of publically owned companies are traded on exchanges such as the NYSE and NASDAQ. They are considered a very liquid investment, as share prices fluctuate minute-by-minute. They can be bought and sold with the click of a mouse on a computer.

Bonds

Bonds can be corporate bonds, municipal bonds or US Treasury bonds. They are debt instruments and represent a fixed income investment in which an investor loans money to a corporation or other entity for a defined period of time at a fixed interest rate. Interest on the bonds is usually paid semi-annually with the full amount of the bond due at maturity. Owners of bonds are called debt holders or bond holders.

One category of bonds I **do not recommend** is called junk bonds. These are non-investment grade bonds paying a high yield. Typically, junk bonds are rated BB or lower by Standard and Poor's. With junk bonds an everyday investor is taking on greater risk. These bonds have a higher default risk, as well. Junk bonds are issued by less creditworthy companies. The risk-reward concept is in full view with junk bonds

Index Funds

These are a special type of mutual fund or they can be an ETF with a portfolio constructed to match or track the components of a market index like the S&P 500. These index funds provide broad market coverage, low operating expenses and have low portfolio turnover. They have been around since late 1975. As the founder of index funds, Jack Bogle, once said, "The honest steward who charges least, wins most. But not for himself, for those investors who entrust their assets to his care. It is not all that complicated." Index funds are a form of passive management.

Exchange Traded Funds (ETFs)

These are market securities that track an index. Unlike a mutual fund, ETFs trade like a common stock. They have been used since 1993. Today, there are some 7,200 ETF products traded worldwide with a market value in assets of $4.8 trillion, according to the London based research firm ETFGI. ETFs may have lower expenses than index funds.

The following asset allocation strategies can give you market rates of return and most investors should be happy with market rates of return. I am talking about index funds and/or ETFs designed like an index fund. Think of it in terms of the tortoise and the hare. The hare sprinted far ahead of the tortoise until he was tired. He stopped to take a nap and rest. The tortoise maintained his slow and steady pace and ultimately won the race. This comparison may help you to better understand these passive investment strategies. Passive is the tortoise; active is the hare. Actively managed investments typically have higher fees than passively managed funds.

The BIG THREE Asset Allocation Strategies

Asset allocation is the process of choosing among different asset categories like stocks, bonds and cash, or all three. Asset allocation is person specific.

Common Stock/Equities

- Index Funds-These will always be "true north" on the compass of investing alternatives. They offer low expense ratios, provide broad diversification and are reasonably tax efficient. Index funds trade like mutual funds.
- Exchange Traded Funds (ETFs)-The same advantages as index funds. ETFs add an additional advantage of even lower fees than some index funds. ETFs trade like stocks.

Bond Funds

- Bond Funds – These invest in debt instruments of the entities on which it is focused (government, corporate, municipal or convertible bonds). Value is expressed as net asset values (NAV). Bond fund expenses have been declining and should not exceed 0.75%. I do not recommend individual bonds for everyday investors. I prefer the corporate bond funds with a small mix of US government bonds or notes.

Cash Reserves

- Cash Reserves-Always maintain some cash in reserve for unique buying opportunities due to any anomaly in the market. A 5% cash reserve may be adequate. The 5% is calculated on the total value of your investment portfolio. Cash is not held as a downside risk protection; rather, it is a readily available source of funds for market opportunities.

The Pension Protection Act of 2006 created the opportunity for an employer to automatically enroll new employees in a company's 401(k) plan, unless the employee chose to opt out of the investment. It also fostered the creation of so called target date funds or life cycle funds. What are the pros and cons of automatic enrollment and target date funds?

Pros – The automatic enrollment simplifies the decision making to get started in a 401(k) plan. This automatic provision should increase the percentage of employees participating in a plan. This feature is best suited for younger employees, as they have time on their side to grow their retirement funds. I encourage you to take advantage of this feature, if your employer offers it. I do not see any negative effects from this employer action.

Cons – Target date funds are too conservative for my tastes. They adjust the allocation between fixed income and equities based on a pre-established age formula or the length of time until you reach full retirement age (FRA). They also charge higher fees than most index funds. I am not a proponent of target date funds, as I think you can do better. Many target date funds are called "robo advised" funds. This means the asset allocation process is executed by a computer (untouched by human hands) based on a participant's age and years before reaching full retirement age.

When I talk about being a long-term investor, what do I mean? In simple terms I can summarize my definition of a long-term investor like this:

- When you focus on the long-term financial returns of your investments, you accept the fact that short and mid-term risks of price swings are unavoidable.
- The old rule that states "100 minus your age is the appropriate allocation percentage for stocks" is an excellent starting point for long-term investors. If you vary this percentage by very much, you are at peril of significant negative consequences for the long-term value of your investment portfolio. It is only a starting point, however. Some investors prefer a lower percentage of bonds and a higher percentage of stocks. The allocation is up to you. Remember, to match your risk tolerance with the asset allocation.
- When the stock market declines or has a major correction of 10% or more, as it will from time to time, you should not sell; look for opportunities to buy additional stocks. Buy on the dips in the

market. I have found the best long-term strategy is to stay fully invested in markets up or down. This approach may test your risk tolerance. Of course, if you need the funds for an emergency, you may have no choice but to sell.

- I define a long-term investor as someone who has a 20 year horizon, or longer. How many years do you have before you reach full retirement age (FRA)? That will be **your** time horizon.
- Long-term investors realize there is no such thing as perfection in the market.

As we get older, most of us narrow our focus to the things that matter most to us. For me, when it comes to investing, my focus is on low expenses, achieving market matching performance, broad diversification, tax efficiency and the ability to invest on an automatic, periodic basis. Minimizing costs has proven to be a winning strategy.

Now that you have mastered the fundamentals of investing, it is time to put them to work building wealth for you. Remember, I am not advising everyday investors to own individual stocks or bonds

A cautionary note: The past performance of the market or a specific index does not guarantee future results.

ELEVEN PRIMARY SECTORS OF THE MARKET[10]

From S & P 500 Index

1. Technology
2. Energy
3. Materials
4. Telecom
5. Financials
6. Industrials
7. Health Care
8. Utilities
9. Consumer Discretionary
10. Real Estate
11. Consumer Staples

---

[10] S & P 500 Index Sectors, www.thebalance.com

According to Bloomberg, the privately owned financial software, data and media company with headquarters in New York City, individual S&P sector performance may vary widely. Over the last ten (10) years, the average difference between the best and worst performing sectors has been more than thirty percent (30%) per year.

There is no pattern or predictability for any of the eleven (11) sectors from year to year. For example, the best and worst sectors ranked by total return over the last five (5) years are listed here, along with their annual returns.

Best and Worst S&P Sector Performance

Year	Best	Worst
2017	Technology 34.28%	Energy (1.06)%
2016	Energy 28.01%	HealthCare (2.83)%
2015	Consumer Discretionary 9.94%	Energy (21.46)%
2014	Utilities 28.59%	Energy (8.60)%
2013	Consumer Discretionary 42.72%	Utilities 13.00%

Compare these wild gyrations of individual sector performance with the overall performance of the S&P 500 Index.

Total S&P 500 Index Performance

One Year (1)	21.83%
Three Year	11.40%
Five Year	15.78%
Ten Year	8.49%

(1) As of December 31, 2017

There are a lot of different ways to dissect and slice the market. For purposes of education and sharing of information, I want you to be aware of some of these differences. When it comes time to select the best investment strategy for you, having this knowledge will be beneficial. The better informed you are, the better decisions you will make. Investment strategies can overwhelm everyday investors with too much data and not enough useful information

PART III

SOLVING LIFE'S BIGGEST FINANCIAL PROBLEMS

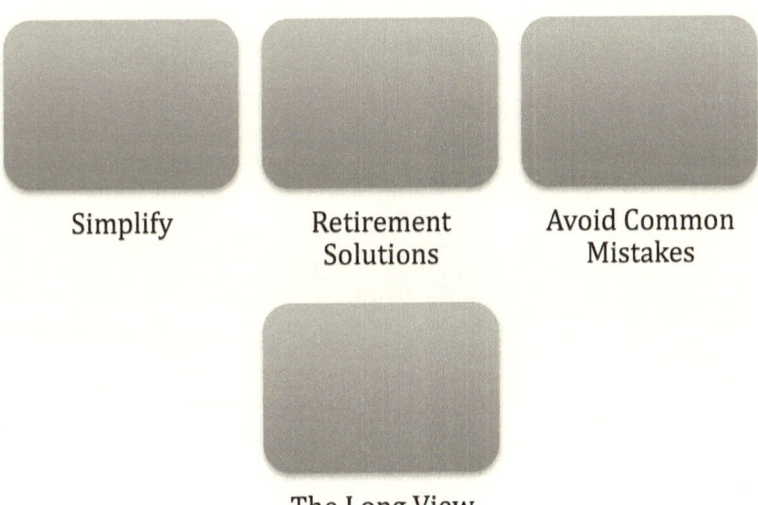

Simplify

Retirement
Solutions

Avoid Common
Mistakes

The Long View

9

SIMPLIFY – SIMPLIFY – SIMPLIFY

Sometimes, the most complicated thing to do is to simplify. Bad habits are hard to break!

> The happiest people do not necessarily
> Have the "Best" things.
> They simply appreciate the things they have.
>
> Warren Buffett

You have probably heard this phrase before. The most important factor in determining the price of real estate is said to be "location-location-location." Something similar can be said about investing and the resultant record keeping that comes with it. One of the important components to successful investing is simplify-simplify-simplify. Hopefully, this is not a new concept for you.

Feeling overcommitted, overextended, too tired to take on another project? You are just like so many other Americans who find themselves overwhelmed with multitasking and trying to navigate successfully between career and family life. You are a prime candidate to simplify. Start with learning to say NO.

Early in my banking career, I read about many different investment strategies. I wanted to try different ones to determine what worked best for me. After all, we all learn from experience. I looked at various investment approaches as a learning experience. At a minimum, I thought this approach might offer me a form of diversification. I opened an account with a bank for an IRA, a separate account for a spousal IRA, maybe a brokerage account for trading and even a mutual fund account with one of the prominent companies in the business. I bought the occasional individual stock being promoted by a stockbroker.

I was in the early stages of my career with a young family, a mortgage and living expenses that consumed most of my net earnings. Usually, each new account I opened only had a small dollar balance consisting of the minimum amount required to open the account. I did not have extra funds to spare. Over time I added small amounts to these accounts when I had a few more dollars. No, this arrangement did not provide the type of diversification I recommend. I also lost money on some of the individual stocks. They were good for the stockbroker (commissions) and bad for me (I lost money).

My advice: make things easier; abridge; shorten; reduce to bare bones; declutter and simplify. This is my motto today. Simplify-Simplify-Simplify. There is no need for so many different accounts or all of the paperwork that comes with their full disclosure, annual privacy policies and monthly statements. The paperwork today can be replaced by digital or electronic copies or by continuing to receive actual paper documentation, if you choose. Both forms of documentation still require reading and time for filing.

In the beginning each account mailed a monthly paper statement to me. Just filing and keeping up with this avalanche of paper became a chore. It was difficult to get a total picture of my investment portfolio with so many, small and diverse accounts. One day I decided to consolidate most of these accounts into two categories: taxable accounts and tax deferred accounts. In the taxable account I included bank accounts and investment accounts on which I paid capital gains or tax on the dividends. In the tax deferred category I maintained various IRA accounts and the 401(k) account I had with my employer. My life took a turn for the better. I had more time to study the market rather than spend time fooling with the paperwork. What a sense of relief.

I still continue to look for ways to simplify my investment accounts and record keeping. The growth of on-line and digital record keeping has made my journey smoother. Storing files on "the cloud" has freed up drawer space. If you are like me, you have multiple saving and investment accounts that you could consolidate and simplify your life. Electronic record keeping has been a big time saver with 24/7/365 availability.

Here is my checklist of eight (8) action steps to assist you in simplifying the investment process and record keeping. I call this my KIS Principle (Keep It Simple).

KIS Principle

- Consolidate accounts
- Have a goal with a set dollar amount for achieving each goal
- Choose passive investment management
- Automate the investment funding process; go on autopilot
- Use index funds or ETFs that track broad markets for diversification
- Maximize both IRA and 401(k) annual contributions
- Rebalance annually or opportunistically
- Utilize electronic record keeping

Follow the KIS Principle (Keep it Simple) to maintain your investment sanity and continue to grow along the road to building wealth. I know my life took a turn for the better when I did.

The KIS Principle

When I talk about consolidating accounts, I mean you only need one IRA, one spousal IRA and one 401(k) account. When you change jobs and leave one employer for another, I recommend moving your old 401(k) account into your existing IRA. This is called a rollover IRA and can be done on a tax-free basis. Be sure to follow the very specific rules for IRA rollovers to avoid any penalties.

The one exception to this consolidation recommendation might be if you have the ability to borrow under your old 401(k) plan. If you think there might be a reason to borrow in the near future, this ability to borrow feature may be very important to you. Many 401(k) plans allow participants the option to borrow against their retirement savings account without penalty, up to a limit. You cannot borrow from an IRA. I do not advise borrowing from any retirement account unless it fills a special need that is unique with your circumstances. In this one case, you may want to maintain the old 401(k) account that allows borrowing.

The idea of establishing a specific dollar amount for each goal is to have a clear definition of what success will look like when you have reached that goal. How will you know if you have met your goal if you do not have a dollar target? After all, you cannot win a race if there is no finish line!

Passive Investing

This is my go-to choice for everyday investors. Choosing passive investment management will help keep investment expenses to a minimum. There are other reasons to adopt the passive investing strategy, as well.

A seismic shift has quietly been underway on Wall Street over the past 10 years. Stocks and bonds still fluctuate in price everyday but the way individual investors hold these assets has changed dramatically.

Passive investing, in which an investor owns a fund or ETF that mimics an index like the S&P 500, has gained popularity over active management, in which the manager selects the portfolio holdings in an attempt to out perform the market.

The father of passive investment management is Jack Bogle, the founder and former CEO of Vanguard Group. Vanguard's ownership is called a mutual structure, in which its various fund shareholders own the firm. This is considered a unique structure within the asset management industry. This has allowed the fees charged by Vanguard to be some of the lowest in the industry. Vanguard Group's assets under management have grown in excess of $5.0 trillion at the end of 2017.

In my opinion, passive investing has the following key advantages:

- Better risk-adjusted returns (broad diversification)
- Greater tax efficiency (less frequent trading)
- Lower fees and expenses (expense ratio)

After choosing the passive investment management strategy, the next step is to consistently add funds to your investment accounts. One of the best ways to accomplish this is by automating the process. I call this putting the fund on autopilot. Setting up an automatic monthly or bi-monthly (twice a month) withdrawal and transfer through your bank or money market fund can complete this process.

A second advantage of adding funds periodically to your investment accounts is the concept of dollar cost averaging. Buying into a basket of market securities with daily fluctuating values will allow you to buy more or less of that investment with each purchase using the same dollars. When the prices are higher than your original purchase, you will buy fewer shares and, conversely, when the prices are lower, you will acquire a larger portion of the investment. This can offer a substantial advantage over time as compared to a one time, lump sum investment in the same fund or index.

Exchange Traded Funds (ETFs)

Exchange traded funds (ETFs) had their inception in 1993, so they are a relatively new concept in investing. People using passive investing strategies dominate ETFs. Money has poured into US index tracking ETFs since 2007. They have become a favorite investment product for both individuals and institutions.

Several differences are clearly documented between index funds and ETFs. The first of these is in the manner of dividend reinvestments. Index funds reinvest dividends automatically, immediately upon receipt of the dividend. ETFs require dividends to be accumulated throughout the quarter and then distributed to the individual shareholders at the end of the quarter. You can buy more ETF shares with the dividends but this is **not** an automatic process. The advantage here is with the index fund.

A second difference is in the area of taxation. ETFs feature an in-kind redemption feature that eliminates the need to sell securities and, therefore, avoid capital gains taxes. This does not work the same way with index funds. In order for an index fund to redeem a security, it must sell the security and you pay any capital gains tax due. In this way, the advantage lies with ETFs.

I like both index funds and ETFs. I use both. This is an area of personal preference. It does not need to be an either or decision. Using both may help you reach your various investment goals more quickly.

Our individual lifestyles are ultimately the representation of a series of routines that we have performed overtime. We become comfortable with these routines and they become habits. Investing and the pursuit of wealth building is another routine to add to your daily life. Do not attempt to "get rich quick" or become a "day trader", as both are a formula for disaster. Keep your day job and select just a few investments as outlined in Chapter 16. Live your investment purpose through your daily life.

As discussed in Chapter 4, do not over complicate your life. Follow the KIS Principle and keep yourself on track to meet your financial goals by following these five (5) recommendations:

- Use index funds and/or ETFs
- Maximize IRA and 401(k) annual contributions
- Rebalance annually in accordance with your pre-determined asset allocation (stock percentage, bond percentage and cash reserve percentage)
- Utilize electronic record keeping
- Simplify not only the paperwork and record keeping but also the investment process

Simplify – Simplify – Simplify! These three words should become your new daily mantra! A mantra is like a slogan, a group of words or a single word that gives you the self-motivation to achieve a very specific goal. Think of a mantra as a dose of medicine for the soul. By using simplify-simplify-simplify as a mantra you may be able to shift old, negative habits into new, positive ones. Repeat these three words often throughout the day. Simplify-Simplify-Simplify

10

SOLVE THE RETIREMENT CONUNDRUM

This is the REALLY BIG ONE! Get it right and you will enjoy retirement. Get it wrong and you will suffer financially and deprive yourself of becoming financially independent.

If you fear you are running behind schedule in funding your retirement accounts, you are not alone. So are a lot of other people. But this is one of those times when misery should not enjoy the company of others. Do not follow the herd! You must break out of this lagging group and face your retirement challenge head-on. Don't be mad, get even and catch up on funding your retirement accounts.

Of all the long-term financial goals you may have, none are any larger in dollar terms or more important than retirement planning. If you get this one right, everything else financially will fall into place. Each of us needs to face the challenge of retirement, as we all will eventually retire. Will you be ready?

Wealth building to fund a retirement nest egg can result in the growth of the largest pool of money or asset you will own during your lifetime. Your retirement account balances should far exceed the value of your home, which some financial professionals have professed will be the largest asset you own.

I am going to debunk the concept that a home is the largest asset to be owned by most families. Your retirement accounts should become the largest asset owned in your family, as you will have to live 25-30 years relying on this source of funds. This will take a lot of money. If you start early, contribute often and maintain financial discipline in funding your retirement accounts, they will become your largest, single asset.

According to a recent study by The Pew Charitable Trusts, the share of private-sector workers who lack access to retirement plans through their employer is 42%. The majority of these employees (78%) work for smaller companies with less than 10 employees. The 42% is an appalling number! Things need to change to make retirement more affordable and possible for the majority of workers.

In the summer of 2017 Oregon became the first state to require employers that do not offer retirement plans of their own to give their employees access to a state-run plan. Oregon is automatically enrolling these private sector employees into Individual Retirement Accounts (IRA) that will be invested in mutual funds run by a third party asset manager. Eight other states are exploring similar programs.

The purpose of these alternative retirement plans is to lessen the burden on state taxpayers over the long term by reducing future retirees' reliance on public assistance programs like Medicaid and others. Employees always have the right to opt-out of these plans.

It is too early to evaluate the success of this approach to retirement planning. At a minimum, it is a step in the right direction and it is being done because it is the right thing to do. Hopefully, this will work satisfactorily for all parties involved.

The reason your retirement funding takes on such a high priority is the fact you will need to live on these funds for 25-30 years (FRA 67 to age 95 = 28 years). Perhaps even longer, if you retire early. Focus on your retirement investing by observing the following:

- Make saving/investing for retirement your No. 1 financial goal.
- Growth stocks/ETFs/index funds should be the primary investments, but some income along the way is nice. Consider an allocation of 70% stocks and 30% bonds, for example.
- Avoid investing in the three C's: currencies, commodities and collectibles as these are too speculative for our more conservative funding strategy.
- Become a no-frills, bottom line, results oriented investor with purpose.

I have narrowed down all of the excuses I have heard over the years from seminar participants about the reasons they have underfunded retirement accounts. These are the three most common excuses:

1. **Late Out of the Gate**: This is better known as not starting to save for retirement sooner. This is the Number One mistake mentioned most often. This is all about missing the early advantages of putting compound interest to work for you growing your retirement nest egg. Here are two examples assuming you were to invest $500.00 per month. The one variable is the start date or the beginning age to invest. The assumed annual rate of return is the same in both examples.

Assume 7.0% return beginning age 25 (40 years)

AGE	BALANCE
25	$6,225
35	86,009
45	255,203
55	588,032
65	1,242,758

Assume 7.0% return beginning age 35 (30 years)

AGE	BALANCE
35	$6,225
45	86,009
55	255,203
65	588,032

2. **Rope, Belt and Suspenders**: This is the tendency to invest too conservatively by restricting investments to US government obligations or FDIC insured bank products. Look at this example

of the impact on the final dollar amount available for retirement, based on a fear of the stock market.

Assume 4.0% return beginning age 25 (40 years)

AGE	BALANCE
25	$6,129
35	73,588
45	182,516
55	343,757
65	582,432

3. **Taking the Retirement Plunge**: If you like to play card games, this might be known as going all in! Moving from a full time job (40 hours per week) directly into full retirement may sound wonderful but it has proven to be a disaster for many. Your mind and body need a transition time to adjust to the many changes that occur in retirement. I encourage you to consider a gradual transition from full time work by easing yourself into retirement. Think in terms of dipping your toe into the water rather than taking a full, headfirst plunge. Reducing working hours and/or fewer days per week worked, being actively involved in volunteer work, starting a part time job and/or consulting in early retirement, may offer a better solution for many retiring adults. Having a meaningful commitment of your time to activities you enjoy has been helpful for some retirees upon leaving the work force.

4. **Summary**: The tables above clearly show the advantages of starting saving/investing at an early age and remaining consistent through the years with adding savings dollars over time. The positive power of compound interest cannot be denied! A retirement nest egg of $1,242,758, as shown in the first example, is a very comfortable way to enter retirement.

One question I am often asked is "how much money will I need in retirement?" Of course, I cannot answer this question because it depends. It depends on your anticipated lifestyle in retirement, it depends on your health and the health of your spouse and other loved ones and it depends on where you plan to live and whether you will work part-time in retirement to supplement your retirement savings. The variables are too numerous to generalize one answer for everyone.

A few years ago Fidelity Investments published a Retirement Savings Guideline that I often refer friends to for a general answer to the question of "how much money will I need in retirement?" This is only a general recommendation, as it cannot answer your specific question without knowing the answer to those questions I posed earlier. So I caution you to remember this is a generic savings guide.

FIDELITY INVESTMENTS
RETIREMENT SAVINGS GUIDELINE[11]

CURRENT AGE	MULTIPLY X SALARY
35	1X
40	2X
45	3X
50	4X
55	5X
60	6X
65	7X
67	8X

For example at age 67 (FRA), if your gross salary is $50,000, you should have saved in your combined retirement accounts (IRA plus 401(k) and any other taxable retirement accounts at least $400,000 (50,000 x 8=$400,000). This is in addition to what you may receive from social security. So use this guideline as a general rule of thumb to compare where you are in saving for retirement. It may also help you determine your current funding gap.

Here is another way to measure your progress toward achieving your retirement goals. To determine how much money you will need in retirement, estimate what income you will need annually and multiply times 25. This is

---

[11] Fidelity Retirement Guideline, www.fidelity.com

how this might work. Again, this is very general and does not include social security.

RETIREMENT NEST EGG ESTIMATOR[12]

ANNUAL AMOUNT EXPECTED TO SPEND	MULTIPLY X 25	ESTIMATED NEST EGG NEEDED
$60,000	X25	$1,500,000
90,000	X25	2,250,000
120,000	X25	3,000,000

Let's check the math on how this might work in reality. If you are comfortable taking 4.0% annual distributions from your total retirement accounts after you reach FRA, the $1,500,000 nest egg will generate $60,000 annually or $5,000 per month. ($1,500,000 x 4.0% = 60,000) The same for the $3,000,000 nest egg. It will generate $120,000 annually or $10,000 per month. ($3,000,000 x 4.0% = 120,000) I think this is a reasonably good estimator for the size of retirement nest egg you will need to generate for the desired amount of income. It does support a 4.0% withdrawal rate.

Another excellent resource for retirement planning questions is AARP's website, aarp.org. When you go to this website, search for Retirement Nest Egg Calculator. This is a generic or basic calculator that will ask for a few inputs and then show you an estimate of how much money you need to live a secure retirement. These are only estimates but this website will give you a number that you can use as a goal. In general, this calculator will estimate you may need as much as 10-12 times your final year's salary to maintain your current lifestyle. Change a few variables and the nest egg amount can change dramatically. Use this website as another tool in helping to solve the retirement conundrum.

The best option to initially stretch your retirement dollars is to delay taking retirement benefits until well past full retirement age. Beginning to draw on social security and your retirement nest egg at age 70 may become the new normal. This assumes you are in good health and can continue working

[12] Fidelity Retirement Estimator, www.fidelity.com

to age 70. Social security has a mandatory requirement for all contributors to begin drawing their benefits no later than age 70.

Other proven ways to stretch your retirement dollars after you retire is to develop multiple sources of income. These might include some or all of the following:

Multiple Sources of Income in Retirement

- Social Security
- Pension
- IRA/401(k) distributions in the form of Required Minimum Distributions (RMD)
- Investment dividends and interest
- Sale of investments with built-in capital gains
- Real Estate income and distributions
- Part-time salary or consulting income
- Become a paid volunteer (to cover expenses)
- Other (use your imagination)

I believe everyone retiring should have at least 3-4 separate income sources. Not only will this improve your cash flow but it will also stretch your retirement funds to last for a longer period of time. Being involved in a business and/or volunteer activities also will keep you socially engaged as well as mentally alert to the needs of others in your community. You have a lot of experience to share with others. This is a win-win for you.

The question of how much money will be needed in retirement is always the most pressing question asked. So I want to give you one additional guideline. According to recent data from the US Census Bureau, there are four (4) factors that reflect the average persons decisions to assist in calculating how much money that average person will need in retirement.

Four Average Factors

1. The average length of retirement is eighteen (18) years.
2. The average retirement age is sixty three (63).

3. The average age most people start to collect social security benefits is sixty two (62).

4. The average social security benefit is $1,404 per month, or almost $17,000 annually.

I do need to remind you these are all averages and none of us are specifically that average person. Your decisions with regard to the above factors will determine your actual results. Another words, the answer to the question of how much money you will need in retirement is still person specific.

If you run the numbers for your individual circumstances and find you are behind where you need to be to have a retirement nest egg sufficient to support your future lifestyle, then catching up on funding your retirement accounts takes on a higher priority.

What should you do about retirement planning if you are actively working in the "gig economy?" Exactly, what is the "gig economy?" As the USA economy continues to evolve, there are more job sharing, ride sharing, and apartment and office space sharing opportunities. It seems people can work from almost anywhere, as long as they have an Internet connection.

Employers are taking advantage of these changes as another way to reduce expenses. Rather than hiring more full time employees (FTE), they are hiring independent contractors for specific, short-term projects. Just like musicians and actors have always worked from gig to gig, now more American workers are beginning to do the same in pursuit of a career. Intuit completed a study on this subject and they have predicted by 2020, up to 40% of workers in the USA could be independent contractors.

As an independent contractor, there are few, if any, benefits offered, other than either a flat sum of money for the project or hourly wages. This means you are all alone when it comes to retirement planning and funding.

I refer you back to Chapter 5, Priorities, where I outlined my seven (7) major priorities for financial wellness. These offer you and your family basic financial protection. You must find a way to cover the expenses for these critical requirements, as well as providing for your retirement.

What about participating in a 401(k) and IRA, as a member of the "gig economy?" As an independent contractor, you do not have access to an employer sponsored 401(k) plan. Either a Roth IRA or traditional IRA can be opened and funded by you, without any concern about where you work. Earned income is the requirement.

Solo 401(k) Plan

The Solo 401(k) or individual 401(k) is a qualified retirement plan for self-employed and their spouses. This applies to independent contractors, as well. The biggest requirement is you must be the owner of your own business. I encourage you to establish a limited liability company (LLC) under the guidelines of your state of legal residency. All income and related business expenses with your independent contractor status should be run through this LLC. Talk with your CPA about the details of what is acceptable business expense for this entity. The costs are minimal to establish a LLC in most states.

Contribution limits are substantially higher for the Solo 401(k) than an employer sponsored plan. In 2018 the annual contributions limits are $55,000. If you are age 50 or older, the limits increase to $61,000. With these limits, building a retirement nest egg can be accelerated.

Setting up a Solo 401(k) does not need to be confusing. I suggest contacting your financial advisor and ask him or her to open a plan for you. Two required documents are needed for a Solo 401(k): Plan Documents, which list a set of options you want included in your plan and Brokerage Documents needed to open an account in the name of the Solo 401(k). Fidelity, Vanguard, TD Ameritrade and E*TRADE all offer prototype plan documents.

I have found over my lifetime of financial experience that these eight (8) generally accepted rules of thumb have relevance in the real world. I share these with you as a way to shorten the time it may take to research some of these topics. Remember, these are only general rules of thumb. Your circumstances may alter the application of these in your life.

Generally Accepted Common Beliefs

1. Buy a house=price should not exceed 2 ½ times your annual income; do not buy the most expensive house in your neighborhood
2. How much to save=at least 10%-15% of annual income just for retirement
3. Stock vs. bonds allocation=Stock portfolio equals same percentage as 100 minus your age; balance of investments held in bonds; very conservative approach

4. Retirement withdrawal rate=3-4% rule adjusted for inflation; stop adjusting for inflation if the value of your retirement portfolio is declining
5. Stock market return=historical return of almost 10% over time
6. Emergency funds= 3-6 months of expenses
7. Pay off credit cards debt= pay from highest interest rate to lowest
8. Buy life insurance=at least 5x gross salary for financial security; may use a combination of term and whole life insurance; spouse should also be insured

Once you reach full retirement age (FRA), your emphasis should shift from the accumulation of assets to an income drawdown strategy. What do I mean by income drawdown? This is a method of withdrawing funds during retirement from investments, IRAs and 401(k) accounts and any insurance products. The idea is to use these retirement funds to provide you with a regular income for the rest of your life.

Here are some suggestions for the withdrawal of funds from various sources after you have retired.

Income Drawdown Strategy

1. Cash and other bank accounts – Use these funds as needed for everyday expenses. No tax due on cash withdrawals but any interest earned on savings or money market accounts will be subject to ordinary income taxes.
2. Part Time Job – If you have a part time job, any earnings from this work may be taxable income. I encourage you to seek part time employment as one method of extending your retirement funds and staying engaged in the business world.
3. Company Pension – If you are lucky enough to have one of these, count yourself among the blessed few who still has access to these company sponsored benefits. The income from most corporate pension plans is taxable. Military pensions and disability pensions may be either partially taxed or tax-free. Check with your tax preparer.

4. Social Security – These monthly benefits are payable for life. They are another form of an annuity with the backing of the full faith and credit of the US government. The maximum amount of benefits that is subject to tax is 85%. There are lower percentages subject to tax depending on your income. Think of your social security benefits as part of your fixed income allocation.

5. Individual Retirement Account (IRA) – If you have a traditional IRA, any withdrawal amount is subject to ordinary income tax. At age 70 ½, you must begin taking a required minimum distribution (RMD). The amount changes annually, based on a longevity table issued by the Internal Revenue Service (IRS). I recommend taking no more than the RMD annually to extend the balance. If you fail to take the annual RMD, you will be subject to a severe penalty.

    For a Roth IRA the withdrawal rules are different. There are no required minimum distributions (RMD) with a Roth. Also, any withdrawal from a Roth is tax-free.

    Managing the withdrawal rate from both traditional IRAs and Roth IRAs is very important. This one factor may have a larger impact than any other on how long your retirement funds can support you in retirement. I recommend a withdrawal rate of 4.0% or less. The RMD may exceed this percentage, but the RMD is a required distribution and must be taken.

6. 401(k) Account – After you leave your last place of employment, I recommend you move any and all 401(k) balances with a tax-free rollover into your existing IRA.

7. Taxable Investment Accounts – Any interest or dividends from these accounts will be subject to tax, as well as a capital gain tax when sold on any appreciation. This also includes bank certificates of deposit with any interest earned subject to ordinary income tax rates.

8. Immediate Annuity – This is an insurance product. It is a form of longevity insurance. When you deposit a lump sum with the insurance company, they agree to pay you a fixed amount every month for life. There are at least five (5) kinds of risks with all annuities. The first is the credit risk of the company issuing the annuity. Second is an inflation risk that will decrease the purchasing power of the annuity payment, if the USA were to enter a period

of high inflation. The third risk is lack of liquidity. Annuity lump sum deposits are not refundable. The fourth risk is the likelihood of your early death. If you die within a few years of taking out an annuity, the insurance company wins, as there are no refunds. If you live longer than the actuarial table predicted when the annuity was issued, then you win. There are ways to mitigate this risk by buying a "period certain" or minimum guaranteed payments. The fifth risk is the lack of flexibility with any annuity. If you needed a lump sum to address some emergency, you cannot get those funds from the annuity. It is a firm contract and cannot be changed. If you can live with these five (5) risks, you might consider taking a portion of your retirement funds, say up to 15-20%, and placing them with an insurance company to buy an immediate annuity. In this way the monthly annuity payment will help offset your living expenses. You will never outlive the annuity. A portion of the payout ratio is tax free as a return of capital while the balance of the monthly payment will be taxable as ordinary income.

9.   Check-a-Month Plan – For anyone uncomfortable turning a lump sum of money over to an insurance company and losing future access to any of those funds, there is another alternative. I call it my check-a-month plan.

The five (5) risks inherent with an immediate annuity are all eliminated with this alternative. The only risk with this alternative is the investment risk inherent with any investment in the market. The best way to execute on my check-a-month plan is **IF** you are working with a financial advisor. You can use this alternative monthly cash flow enhancement as a D-I-Y investor, but to be successful, will require more work on your part.

Ask your financial advisor to develop an income plan generating a fixed amount payable to you monthly. Your advisor will use a portion of your retirement funds for this purpose, just like purchasing an immediate annuity, but without the same risks.

The key to making this work for you is finding a combination of interest, dividends and capital gains to meet your monthly cash flow needs. Payouts under this plan will include some combination of funds subject to ordinary tax, capital gains and return of capital.

The combined tax rate should be lower than the tax rate paid on payments made with an immediate annuity.

Personally, I prefer my check-a-month plan versus the immediate annuity option. Check-a-month offers greater flexibility and the money is always accessible in the event of an emergency. The only drawback to this preference is it that it may not be a guaranteed payment for life. Any guarantee will depend on the size of the total retirement fund. If a guaranteed lifetime payment is what is most important to you, an immediate annuity may be the better option for you.

Because of the low interest rates currently in the market, I do not think this is a good time to purchase an immediate annuity. Current interest rates as well as your age affect the payout ratio for an immediate annuity. Watch for a better opportunity to make this type of purchase in the future, if you can.

Do you want to have a retirement cake and eat it too? Do you want to spend all of your funds during retirement or do you want to leave something to the kids or other beneficiaries? Is it possible to do both? As crazy as it may sound, doing both may be possible!

According to the actuarial firm Millman, Inc, based in Seattle, one-way might be to include an immediate annuity in your retirement accounts. Including the immediate annuity actually increases the amount you can leave to your heirs compared to putting all your money in stock and bond investments according to a Millman study.

Their studies have shown that an immediate annuity on average can provide more lifetime income than an everyday investor can earn from high quality fixed income investments. Because of this greater income feature, the other investments are left untouched in the early years of retirement, thus allowing them to grow to a larger total amount than if retirees were making regular withdrawals to pay their expenses. The larger account balances may make it possible to leave something to your heirs.

My take away from this study is the importance of having enough sources of predictable income, whether it is from immediate annuities, my check-a-month plan or other sources, to cover basic living expenses in the early years of retirement without relying on unpredictable and uncertain investment returns. It may truly be possible to have it both ways.

Retirement planning is always a work in progress. Sometimes it will need a little adjustment for changes in the financial environment or changes in your life. So keep your plan a dynamic plan, making updates and changes, as needed.

A Dirty Dozen Plus One of Retirement Planning Mistakes

In no particular order here are thirteen (13) mistakes that can cost you a lot of money in retirement. Being aware of them is the first step. Avoiding them is the action step. Ignoring them may put your retirement security at risk.

1. **Underestimating how long you will live (the longevity gap).** Recent surveys among people within five (5) years of retirement found that approximately three out of four did not accurately answer the question "how long will a typical 65 year old man expect to live?" The correct answer is at least 20 years. The participant's answers underestimated this by five years or more. This underestimate can cost the retiree another $100,000 or more. If the funding is not there, these additional years may be spent living on meager financial resources. Best to plan on living 25-30 years after reaching full retirement age.

   Living too long can be considered a risk! Longevity has a way of diminishing your retirement account balances and if you live too long, you may out live your funds. This potential development (I consider a long life a blessing not a risk) can be mitigated by actively following the simple strategies outlined in this book.

2. **Underestimating how much to save for retirement (underfunding).** You can see how this is exacerbated by the first mistake listed above. Funding of 401(k) accounts and IRAs is the bedrock for retirement planning **but** it is not enough. You also must save and invest in other retirement accounts to achieve financial freedom in retirement.

3. **Not understanding the power of delaying social security benefits.** While most Americans are eligible to begin drawing social security benefits at age 62, the penalty is rather severe. A reduction of 25% of the monthly benefit is standard and this reduction will continue

for the rest of your life. For those born between 1943 and 1954, full retirement age (FRA) is 66. If you start drawing benefits at age 66, you receive 100% of your monthly benefit. If you delay taking benefits, after FRA, your monthly benefits will continue to grow.

Age 67 = 108%
Age 68 = 116%
Age 69 = 124%
Age 70 = 132%

If you are married, think about the major impact on your combined monthly benefits, if your spouse also delays taking benefits to age 70. This is money on the table, **if** you can plan for this eventuality.

4. **A failure to plan.** If you lack a defined destination, then any place can be where you land. In other words, without a plan, you have no road map for going where you want to go. A Harvard Business School study on goal setting found:

   • 83% do not have clearly defined goals
   • 14% have goals but they are not written down
   • Only 3% have goals committed to writing

   Fortune magazine published a study showing people with written plansend up with an average of five times (5X) the amount of money at retirement as those with no written plan. Need I say more?

5. **Fail to start saving early enough.** This is the classic example of so many adults who do not understand that planning their retirement is their responsibility, not the government, not your employer and not the bank of mom and dad. In my earlier book, *Put Time on Your Side*, I illustrated the importance of starting to save and invest early to take advantage of the power of compounding interest. For every six years you delay starting to save and invest for retirement, you double the dollar amount needed to achieve the same retirement goal.

"You are either saving for retirement today or consuming
your retirement today." Anonymous

6. **Failure to maximize tax deferred investments.** When the burden
for planning and funding your personal retirement plan shifted from
your employer to you, the government provided some attractive
incentives to help you with this financial burden. Earnings and
capital gains in 401(k) and regular IRAs are tax deferred until you
withdraw them at retirement. Earnings in a Roth IRA are tax free
when withdrawn. The deferral of taxes is a major advantage of
these retirement accounts over taxable accounts. Everyday investors
should take advantage of this deferral by contributing the maximum
allowed annually for each 401(k) and IRA.

"Procrastination is the *Thief* of Time."
Edward Young

7. **Work till you drop or they carry you out of the office/factory
toes first.** Too many people believe they will work well past age
70. They enjoy their career and the social interaction it provides.
This belief is strongest among younger workers. However, the aging
process has a way of slowing down, both mentally and physically, the
ability to work at the same productive level as younger employees.
With age come more serious health issues for you and your spouse.
No one can work forever, even when he or she want to. As you age,
relying on income from a job as your primary retirement cash flow
is both foolish and unrealistic.

"We have some control over when we retire. However,
we have very little control over how long we live."
Gordon Smith

8. **Over reliance on Social Security or a company pension plan
(if you are lucky enough to have one).** Social Security was never
meant to be your only source of income in retirement. It was created
as a safety net for senior citizens and those with disabilities to help
cover basic living expenses. Benefits are calculated based on your
individual earnings record. You can contact Social Security for an
estimate of your benefits at any time. In this way your future benefits

will not be a surprise. If you have a company pension, most likely it will be based on a percentage of your earnings over time. Many employer sponsored pension plans are underfunded and future reductions in the payouts may occur. Again, company pensions usually offer a fraction of your preretirement income and should not be the only source of income in retirement. Look for multiple sources of income to help defray the costs of retirement. Calculating social security benefits for spouses (working or non-working) may be different.

9.   **Spend it rather than roll it over.** When you change jobs you have an opportunity to do a tax-free rollover of funds from your previous employers retirement accounts such as a 401(k). There is a 60-day window to transfer these funds without tax into your Individual Retirement Account (IRA). Unfortunately, too many young workers look at the availability of these funds as a windfall (like an unexpected tax refund) and spend these retirement dollars. This is a major mistake, unless there is a pressing health issue or other life or death circumstance. Hewitt Associates completed a study of workers and found, regardless of the age of the participants, 45% of workers cash out rather than rollover to an IRA when changing jobs. This spells disaster for future retirement income withdrawals.

10.   **Investment fees and expenses are too high.** As I have said before, expenses matter for all investment accounts. Even a small 1% additional fee can reduce the total return on an account over time by a significant amount. All fees should be monitored and reviewed on a regular basis. The expense ratio of one index fund can easily be compared to another. Fees should only pay for something of value. If you pay your financial advisor a 1% fee on assets under management (AUM), then the advisor should add more than 1% per year in value compared to passive index funds (net of taxes and all other fees). Keep your focus on your investment total returns and monitor all fees and expenses. You must avoid costs in the form of extra fees without benefits!

11.   **Underestimating total health care costs in retirement.** This can be a really big expense that is hard to estimate. Each individual has a unique set of health issues. Fidelity Investments has estimated an average couple will spend $245,000 over their retirement lives just for **out of pocket** medical expenses. If one or both need nursing home care, this amount may increase by an additional $150,000 or more.

How many retirees are prepared for this potential outcome? Your retirement planning should incorporate some provision for future healthcare expenses. Medicare does not cover 100% of healthcare expenses and the premiums for Medicare keep increasing.

12. **Investing in the wrong products at the wrong time in retirement.** As a retiree, you have time to research all types of investments or to work more closely with your financial advisor to explore different investment alternatives. Beware any advisor who is selling you any product. He gets a commission and you may get stuck with a product you do not need or that is inappropriate for your retirement plan. One product that should not be purchased in retirement is a variable annuity. This is an insurance product that invests in mutual fund like investments. It adds additional market risks to your retirement account. Usually these products have high costs, fees, surrender charges and other expenses. Increased valuations in a variable annuity such as capital gains and dividends are taxed as ordinary income when funds are withdrawn. There are many other products available that allow market gains to be taxed as capital gains, at a much lower rate. Beware adding undue risks and high expenses to your retirement account.

"Experience is the name everyone gives to their mistakes."
Oscar Wilde

13. **Giving financial help to family members.** This is one of the most difficult areas in which to learn to say NO. If you do not, there will be frequent requests. Saying YES can imperil your own retirement. I am specifically talking about adult children and/or relatives of the immediate family. None of us want to see our children or other family members suffer financially but the reality is you are dealing with adults in these examples. You have raised your children, probably helped financially to educate them and provided for their living needs and expenses for a number of years. It is time for them to leave the nest and live on their own.

Unexpected expenses such as a wedding or a second marriage for an adult child (say over 30 years of age or older) should not be the financial responsibility of the parents. As a parent, if you guaranteed some student debt for one of your children and that child defaults on that debt, you are responsible to repay the debt in full. You are on the hook for this one.

Grown children who want to move back home for reasons like separation or divorce, loss of a job or just to save some money, presents another array of problems.

If you have a child needing to move back home for any reason, at a minimum, I suggest you draft an agreement in advance that clearly states how long you will accommodate this arrangement, what expenses will be shared while they are living with you and have a clear understanding of when this arrangement will end. I even suggest you establish a date certain on when they will move out. "You can stay until you get your feet on the ground" is not a date certain. After all, you have been through the lean times and already made financial sacrifices to be able to live comfortably in retirement. Enough is enough!

Retirement is a time for you and your spouse to enjoy time with each other and have some peace and quiet. It is your time to enjoy the present. Do not feel guilty for protecting your retirement dollars and time. If you do not, your retirement funds will be depleted much sooner than you had planned. Who will come to your aid, if that happens?

There you have my list of the thirteen (13) deadly errors that can destroy the value of your retirement accounts. You have worked hard for your money and you should keep your money working just as hard for you in retirement. Avoid undue risks and additional expenses to enjoy a more stress free phase of your life.

One final comment on retirement. I have been asked if a retiree should continue to save? I believe by the time you retire, the savings habit has become a part of who you are. There should be no reason to stop saving, assuming you have adequate income to cover your expenses. What might change in retirement is the amount you save.

Mechanical devices like a car, furnace, air conditioner, washer and dryer and others will continue to wear out or break down. These more costly items do not respect the fact you are in retirement. Household repairs, painting, replace a worn out roof and remodeling to adapt to the needs of aging occupants all will cost money.

I suggest it is a good idea to continue to fund those money buckets you set up earlier for emergencies and living expenses. Emergencies and living expenses will continue until you die. It is better to fund these higher dollar expenses from savings than from withdrawals from your retirement accounts.

At age 70 1/2 and thereafter, you are no longer eligible to contribute to a traditional IRA. Roth IRAs do not have any age limitations on eligibility but they do on income earned. So if you have extra money in retirement, continuing to save seems to make sense. You can even continue to fund a Roth IRA, if you qualify and if that makes financial sense for you.

Time devours all things including life, buildings, civilizations and investment opportunities. Do not let elapsed time close your window of opportunity to provide for a well-funded retirement program. Even for a person who has everything, **time** is still their most precious possession.

Most people only retire once; at some point, their retirement date becomes the beginning of the rest of their life. ("Tomorrow is the first day of the rest of your life!") Why not get it right and enjoy a comfortable financial future based on the good planning and financial discipline you have developed during your working years?

There are only two things that last forever: love and regret. Show your love for your spouse and family and avoid any lasting guilt or regret by providing for a well-funded retirement plan. They will enjoy the benefits for their lifetime, as will you.

Time is only your friend when you start saving early and maintain financial discipline in funding your retirement accounts.

11

AVOID COMMON
INVESTMENT MISTAKES

Who has not made a mistake today, this week or this month? Mistakes are as common as dirt. Some mistakes carry very few consequences like failure to turn the lights off when you leave the house. Another uneventful mistake might be misplacing your keys from their normal resting place on the hook and leaving them in your pocket, instead. Other mistakes can have a major impact on your future.

Just like in your daily activities, some mistakes in the area of investing have the potential to contribute to long-term negative results. If I can help you avoid a few of these mistakes, my belief is you will come out ahead in your investment results. Investment mistakes end up costing you money and that is why I want you to avoid them, when possible.

There are six (6) common investment mistakes that I believe many everyday investors will make in their lifetime. They fall under common themes. These topics are general in nature versus the specific retirement mistakes discussed previously in Chapter 10.

Six Common Mistakes

- Failing to invest
- Trying to time the market rather than spend time in the market
- Changing strategies frequently
- Incurring high investment expenses
- Getting out of the market/ Going to cash/Being slow to re-enter the market
- Over worrying about short-term market fluctuations

Failing to Invest

Being afraid to pull the trigger and invest in the stock and bond market carries a high risk for your future financial well being. Just like a failure in our educational system to invest in better outcomes necessary for a bright future for young students. This would be a mistake condemning millions of young minds to a future lacking in hope. Using a crutch such as lack of knowledge, lacking any specific financial goal, high anxiety and risk avoidance and an overwhelming lack of patience and discipline cannot be an excuse. Previous chapters have outlined how to address these matters. All you need to do is move forward and get involved in the market. After all, fortune favors the bold!

You may be flirting with the law of unintended consequences. Taking no investment action will result in you falling behind in your retirement funding. Underfunded retirement accounts will contribute to a lower standard of living in retirement than you may have anticipated.

Trying to Time the Market

Study after study has proven trying to time the market does not work. By timing the market I mean attempting to predict the future direction of the market or moving in and out of the market by frequently switching asset classes. Market timing is a fool's game. As my old college finance professor said, "Stay fully invested and you will never miss the next bull run in the market."

Changing Strategies Frequently

This mistake typically is more emotionally driven than factually motivated. I am all in favor of rebalancing your portfolio annually, but this is not the same as switching strategies. Any adjustments to your asset allocations should be based on current economic and market conditions, not market movements favoring one sector over another. Avoid this mistake for the benefit of better long-term investment results.

Rebalance serves as a good metaphor for long-term investing. Your long-term plan should provide investment strategies that you can use throughout your life.

Incurring High Investment Expenses

These expenses may be expressed as an expense ratio, meaning the total percentage of fund assets used to cover all expenses of a fund. For passive index funds a typical expense ratio is near 0.25% or lower while actively managed funds tend to have higher expense ratios between 0.5-1.0% plus. One of the keys to successful investing is to keep investment expenses low. After all, one of the important measures for performance is how much money you have left to invest after fees and taxes. Watch investment expenses closely. Just like in golf, the lower the number the better.

Investing in the stock market means you accept that performance fluctuates, it comes and goes over time. Fees, however, are consistent. They eat away your dollars for investment.

Getting Out of the Market/ Going to Cash/Being slow to re-enter the market

Investors who cash out of the market call it going to cash. Everyday investors typically who go to cash get out of the market too late and then compound the problem by waiting too long to get back in the market. Again, this mistake is all about understanding your personal risk tolerance. The most important role for cash is not downside protection but rather the advantage it provides for upside buying opportunities and investment flexibility. Investment time horizon, risk tolerance and emergency cash needs make it impossible for me or anyone else to advise you on the appropriate level of cash to retain. I think a 5% cash reserve should be adequate for most everyday investors.

Over Worrying About Short-Term Market Fluctuations

Short-term market fluctuations are irrelevant, if you are committed to a long-term investment strategy. Most short-term worries are emotionally driven. Market volatility is inevitable. Prices go up and down everyday. The most important valuation for your retirement funds is when you reach full retirement age (FRA). Keep your focus on this future number. Remember the old adage, "You can't make an omelet without breaking a few eggs." Like an omelet, the end product of your investment strategy is what counts. This will be your nest egg for retirement.

A final word on another common mistake. Do not confuse historical returns with future market expectations. Your investment experience is unique to you. When you start investing (at what age), how much you invest, and when do you invest (monthly, quarterly, annually). Do you maintain financial discipline, do you have a large, lump sum investment near retirement age and numerous other factors make your experience one of a kind. These factors make your investment experience different from the historical average performance. You may perform better or worse than the averages.

What does it take to go from having a general awareness of common mistakes to actually changing your financial behavior and avoiding them? Reading books like *Investing 1.0.1 With Purpose* is a place to start to improve your financial literacy. Maintaining financial discipline to fund your retirement plan regularly is another. The best advice is to stay focused on the things you can control. Here are a few activities within each investor's full control that will lead to your improved financial wellness.

Focus On What You Can Control

- Goal Setting
- Follow your long-term retirement plan
- Select low-cost investments
- Rebalance your portfolio annually
- Decide when, where and how much to invest
- Asset allocation does affect long-term performance
- Broad diversification offers a lower risk profile

In addition to staying focused on what you can control, steering clear of just one or two of these common mistakes can make the difference between successful wealth building and ultimately only living on social security in retirement.

12

THE LONG VIEW

Financial advisors, stockbrokers, day traders and even the man in the street all believe they know **the** best stock selection techniques and have **the** investment process all figured out. From *A Random Walk Down Wall Street* by Burton Malkiel published in 1973 to the many quants working at Bridgewater Associates, all of these different "experts" promote a process that makes them money.

I do not earn any fees or receive any compensation from any source based on my investment recommendations. From my more detached view of the markets and my lifetime of financial experience, I recommend only what has worked for me. I believe as an everyday investor, this will work for you, as well.

I am a proponent of the Buy and Hold approach to investing. I believe if you invest in quality companies or index funds/ETFs and monitor their performance over time, this can be a long term winning strategy. What better source of good, quality investments than the US stock and bond markets?

What do I mean when I say Buy and Hold as a strategy? This is a passive investment strategy in which an investor buys stocks and bonds (or indexes and/or ETFs) and holds them for an extended period of time, regardless of market fluctuations such as short-term price movements. Holding investments long enough to qualify for long-term capital gains rates also offers some tax advantages. The long-term capital gains rates are 0-20% in 2018, depending on your personal filing status and AGI. This is a lower rate than the standard tax rate for 2018 on ordinary income for those same filers. The opposite of a Buy and Hold investor is a day trader or computer driven trading based purely on algorithms.

What Buy and Hold **does not mean!** This does not mean you put your investment portfolio on the shelf and forget about it. It does not mean you bury your head in the sand and ignore what is going on in real time in the economy, your community, your state, nation and the world. Being flexible and taking advantage of financial opportunities when they present themselves is still important in building a successful, long-term investment portfolio. Be vigilant, stay tuned in and make adjustments, as needed.

There are some investors and advisors who call this strategy The Long View. What I know is this is the right shape and size strategy for my investing approach for long-term investors. Buy and Hold also lowers the number of transactions in an investment account and that means lower fees and other expenses. Buy and Hold – The Long View is another factor leading to minimal costs and a winning strategy for everyday investors.

One of the factors often credited to the investing success of Warren Buffett, currently the third richest man in the world with a personal net worth of more than $80 billion, is his commitment to long term investing. His Buy and Hold philosophy has worked extremely well for him over the past six decades. It all starts with buying into quality investments.

I have been asked how long is the Long View? My answer is again, it depends. It depends on the individual perspective of the everyday investor. I know the minimum timeframe for me would be 10 years or longer but I do not know an exact answer to the question for everyone.

Along with Buy and Hold, I also advocate a Less-Can-Be-More approach to investing. In my opinion this minimalist strategy can offer at least these five (5) positive results to investors who want to follow this same path.

Less-Can-Be-More

1. Market rates of return
2. Lower costs
3. Limited market risks
4. Broad market diversification
5. Tax efficiency

I believe it is possible to achieve all five of these results by using only 3-4 different investment funds. That is why this is a minimalist strategy. I offer specific investment recommendations in detail in Chapter 16.

Municipal Bonds

I am often asked about municipal bonds and for a specific recommendation in this specialized area of investments. Specifically, "Should municipal bonds be one of my Core holdings?" This is an area of investing I have not previously written about, as I have mixed feelings about the appropriateness of this asset class for everyday investors.

What is a municipal bond? It is a debt security issued by a state, municipality, state agency or county to finance their capital expenditures. Municipal bonds are usually tax free at the Federal tax level and they can be tax free at the state and local level, if the bond is issued by an entity in the state of the legal residency of the investor. I have used selected municipal bonds in the past as one way to reduce volatility, lower my risk profile and increase yield within a given portfolio. I particularly like the triple exempt bonds, as they are exempt from Federal, state and local taxes, assuming they are qualified for all three exemptions.

There are two general classes of municipal bonds: rated and non-rated (investment grade and non-investment grade). I would avoid all non-rated municipal bonds, as they have not passed the financial underwriting tests of various rating agencies such as Moody's and Fitch's. Being non-rated raises the risk level. Within the class of rated municipal bonds, the higher the rating, the lower the assumed potential risks. Aaa is the highest rating and investment grade municipal bonds can be rated as low as Baa or higher.

The traditional method of comparing the return of a municipal bond with a conventional investment held in a taxable account has been to convert the tax free yield of the municipal bond to a tax equivalent yield (TEY). Then it is possible to do an apples to apples comparison of the TEY to the yield of the alternative, taxable investment. For example:

Tax Equivalent Yield (TEY) Calculation

Step #1	Municipal bond yield (tax free) 3.0%
	$\dfrac{\text{Municipal bond yield (tax free) } 3.0\%}{\text{Reciprocal of your personal Tax rate } (1.00 - 0.25) \quad 0.75} = 4.0\%$ TEY Assumes a 25% tax bracket
Step #2	If a taxable bond of the same credit quality AND the same maturity date yields more than 4.0% in this example, then you would earn a higher return on the taxable bond.
Step #3	The higher your personal tax rate, the higher the TEY. Therefore, tax free municipal bonds are usually better choices for individuals in the higher tax brackets.
Step #4	If comparing a tax-free municipal bond issued by an entity in your state of legal residency, then you should also include your marginal state tax rate in determining the TEY. $\dfrac{\text{Muni bond yield } 3.0\%}{\text{Reciprocal} \quad 0.6980} = 4.30\%$ TEY $(1.00 - 25\%\text{-say } 5.2\% = 0.6980)$

As with individual stocks and bonds, there are individual municipal bonds and there are municipal bond funds. These bond funds function similar to stock mutual funds. They spread the risks among the pool of bonds in the fund. They also seek to provide a high level of current income exempt from Federal tax. They may or may not qualify for your state tax exemption. Read the details of the bond fund description very carefully for full disclosure.

General Obligation Bonds

The taxing authority of the issuer backs general obligation bonds. These municipal bonds, known as GOs, are considered to be safer than other types of municipal bonds. The issuer has the power to levy taxes on residents and this power lowers the potential risk of default.

Revenue Bonds

These municipal bonds are used to finance specific public projects and are backed only by the revenue generated by the specific project being financed. They are considered less safe than general obligation bonds. If the project does not generate sufficient revenue, the total project may default.

There are a number of municipal bond funds to choose from. Here are a few of the larger funds:

- American High Income Municipal Bond Fund (AMHIX): This fund has an upfront sales charge known as a load. It is considered to have an above average expense ratio (more expensive). The net expense ratio is 0.67% ($6.70/1000 invested)
- Vanguard Intermediate Term Tax Exempt Fund (VWITX): This is a no load fund meaning there is no upfront sales charge. The expense ratio is considered to be low (less expensive). The net expense ratio is 0.19% ($1.90/ 1000 invested).
- Fidelity Tax-Free Bond Fund (FTABK): This is a no load fund with a low expense ratio of 0.25 ($2.50/1000 invested).

On a historical basis, the default rate for A rated or better municipal bonds has been low (estimated around 0.30%). However, I believe **the risks have increased** since the 2008 financial crisis. Defaults, payment problems and even bankruptcy have increased in frequency among some municipal bond issuers.

Here is a short list of some of the bankruptcy filings of municipal bond issuers in the recent past.

Recent Bankrupt Municipal Bond Issuers

Jefferson City, AL
Central Hills, RI
Detroit, MI
San Bernardino, CA
Stockton, CA
Harrisburg, PA

Housing, hospitals, healthcare and infrastructure have been some of the most common sectors to default. Potentially add to this list the pending financial crisis developing in Puerto Rico resulting from the 2017 disaster caused by Hurricane Maria. It is uncertain at this time how Puerto Rico and their municipal bond issuers will manage to meet the obligations for pending interest payments and maturities coming due on some of their bonds. There is increasing risk with these bonds.

Many of the problems facing some of the government entities issuing municipal bonds originates from their failure to control spending while taxpayers resist higher taxes within some of these states. When the gap between revenue and expenses widens, municipal bonds may feel the pressure to delay, default or reorganize their financial obligations. The municipal bond debt holders may suffer the consequences.

The largest on-going problem facing many states, cities and counties in the USA is the large dollar amount of **unfunded and/or underfunded pension liabilities** they face in meeting the current and future retirement costs of their employees. This unfunded liability also puts pressure on the financial well being of these various state government entities that issue municipal bonds.

States are usually considered to be a safer issuer of municipal bonds than agencies. This is because of their ability to raise revenues through tax increases and their inability to file for bankruptcy protection. The Federal bankruptcy code says that individuals, corporations and municipalities may file bankruptcy but no Federal law allows a state to file bankruptcy. Unless Congress was to amend the Constitution, this prohibition for states should stand the test of time. No state has defaulted on its general obligation bonds since Arkansas in 1933.

Should municipal bonds be part of the Core holdings for everyday investors?

NO, I do not recommend municipal bonds for one of your Core holdings. The risks are rising faster than the tax equivalent yields (TEY). I believe you will be better served as a long-term investor with taxable investments held outside of your Individual Retirement Accounts (IRAs) and 401(k) accounts.

Here are a couple of random thoughts that you might be able to use in your financial planning.

- **Personal gift tax exclusion.** In 2018 the individual gift tax exclusion was increased from $14,000 to 15,000 per person. This would mean a couple could give up to $30,000 annually to the same person, without any tax consequences. This amount would go a long way in helping a grandchild with college expenses, for example. Over 5 years, this could be as much as $150,000 transferred to one person. This can be a powerful planning tool.

- **Estate tax exemption.** The estate tax exemption was increased in 2018 to $11,200,000 per person from 5,490,000. This will allow more people to leave their estate to their beneficiaries without worrying about estate taxes eating into their final bequests. This is a big increase in the exemption that will benefit many individuals, as well as small business and family farm owners.

Here is an idea that any long-term investor can use, particularly members of the millennial generation. For as little as $5,000 invested every year, it is possible to amass a $1,000,000 nest egg or more for retirement. Here is how this might work.

Historically, the USA stock market has basically doubled every 10-12 years since 1960 because the economy has doubled over those same 10-12 year periods. The S&P 500 Index has had a total return since 2000 of 78.785%, with dividends reinvested and adjusted for inflation. Starting with a ZERO investment and adding $5,000 annually to an investment in the S&P 500 Index, it is possible to generate $1,000,000 or more by age 67(FRA). Assume a millennial starts an investment program as simple as putting $5,000 a year in the S&P 500 index at age 27. His or her full retirement age is 67. Follow the potential investment results in the chart below.

Build a $1,000,000 Nest Egg With a $5,000 Annual Investment Over Time

Annual Return	Final Nest Egg $$$$ (40 years)
5.0%	634,199
6.0%	820,238
7.0%	1,068,048
8.0%	1,398,905
9.0%	1,841,459
10.0%	2,434,259

A Buy and Hold strategy combined with $5,000 invested annually can be a very powerful idea in building wealth for the future. ($5,000 divided by 12 =

$420 per month or $14 per day invested for your future.) The S&P 500 Index offers a broad diversification of large cap stocks, as well as a low expense ratio when using one of the platforms available from Fidelity, Vanguard, Schwab or E*Trade, to mention a few.

The Long View is still very relevant to your purpose in building wealth for the future. A Buy and Hold strategy utilizing a Less-Can-Be-More approach just makes sense for most everyday investors.

The Long View does not follow the clock. Time is measured in years and decades, not days and hours.

PART IV

NO MORE FINANCIAL WORRIES

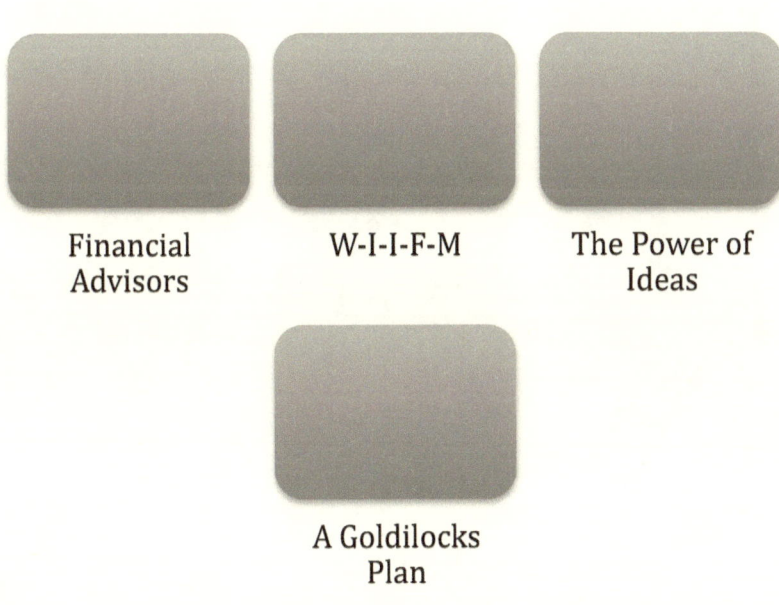

Financial
Advisors

W-I-I-F-M

The Power of
Ideas

A Goldilocks
Plan

13

FINANCIAL ADVISORS

Throughout this book I have talked a lot about do-it-yourself (D-I-Y) investing. I know many of you do not feel comfortable undertaking this life-changing project on your own. That is why I have included this chapter on financial advisors.

Do you need a financial advisor? The answer depends on your level of financial training/experience and self-confidence in your ability to make investment decisions. You may not need an advisor when you start, but I believe most everyday investors will need an advisor before they complete the journey on the road leading to wealth building. This is why I include this tropic in this section on No More Financial Worries.

By financial advisor I do not mean a stockbroker or a bond salesman. I am recommending a licensed registered investment advisor (RIA) with a Certified Financial Planner (CFP) or Chartered Financial Analyst (CFA), or another specialized designation. These advisors work on a fee basis only, based on assets under management (AUM). They are subject to the fiduciary rule and are required to work in the best interests of their clients. Failure to do so is grounds for dismissal and serious monetary fines.

Any financial advisor who manages your money should be a Registered Investment Advisor (RIA).[13]

As you can probably tell, I am a strong proponent of passive index/ETF investing for everyday investors. More on the specifics of this strategy are detailed in Chapter 16. If you are following my advice, you know it is easy for an individual to begin the investing process with an index fund and/or ETF as a D-I-Y investor.

Beginning on your own is made easy by the availability of many on-line stock-trading platforms. Pick an index with a broad diversified, market group of stocks and get started. My default index fund is the SPDR S&P 500 ETF (symbol is SPY). The current expense ratio for this fund is 0.09% and it began trading in 1993. ETFs have no required minimum investment. You can buy as much or as little as you want just by placing an order through your on-line brokerage account under the symbol SPY.

I think this is a good way to get started. You can stay with this D-I-Y approach until you have at least $100,000 accumulated in this account. At that point, I recommend you seek the advice of a financial advisor. They will be quick to point out whatever their minimum assets under management (AUM) threshold may be. They will discuss their fee structure, as well. They will ask you to articulate your personal investment philosophy. You decide if working with a financial advisor is best for you.

My best advice on how to find a financial advisor is by talking with friends and associates. Who do they use, why, are they satisfied with the fee structure and do they recommend this advisor for you? A recommendation from a trusted friend or satisfied customer carries a lot of weight with me.

I am personally drawn to an advisor who clearly focuses on the basics. Also, insights into recent changes that affect retirement planning and estate planning are invaluable. As important as these two components are, the overriding quality I seek is a clear, concise communicator. I want my advisor to be a voice of calm and reason during an otherwise sometime anxious financial market.

At the end of the day, even though I am paying a fee for services rendered by my financial advisor, I recognize the personal responsibility I have for my own wealth-building plan. I provide my input at every opportunity.

---

[13] Registered Investment Advisors must be registered with the federal Securities and Exchange Commission or the state securities office where they do business and this entitles them to give personal investment advice.

Here is some solid advice from three current financial advisors on how to find and select a financial advisor. Remember, personal compatibility is one of the most important components of working with a financial advisor. Compatibility is the ultimate litmus test.

Advisor #1

1. Prioritize what you are looking for from an advisor?
    -   Investment advice only
    -   Financial planning such as budgeting, debt reduction, asset protection, etc
    -   Wealth management to include investments, planning, cash flow management, taxes, estate planning, etc
2. Use friends, family and social networks to find a compatible advisor who has worked with someone you know and respect. These referrals help to reduce turnover as they come with similar needs and expectations as the current clients of the advisor

Advisor #2

1. Always work with a fiduciary and someone who has to legally work in your best interest
2. Conduct due diligence by at a minimum doing a background check on the advisor and the firm with the SEC: http://www.adviserinfo. sec.gov/
3. Review the firm's legal disclosures such as Form ADV
4. Seek advice and avoid purchasing products such as life insurance or annuities directly from the advisor.
5. Research credentials. Everyone in the industry calls himself or herself a financial adviser. What are their qualifications? Do they have an advanced degree or meaningful industry designation such as a CFP or CFA?
6. Never purchase a product that is opaque or you do not understand. Private placement non-public investments are notorious for Ponzi schemes and charlatans.
7. Ask for references.

8. If it sounds too good to be true, it probably is! There is no silver bullet in investing. If someone holds himself or herself out to have some secret sauce that can predict the market or always beat the market, alarm bells should definitely go off. The only investor I know who consistently produced 8% returns with little or no volatility was Bernie Madoff***.

9. Seek second opinions before finalizing a decision. Doctors are not infallible and neither are financial advisors.

10. Listen to Warren Buffett. He is one of the best long-term investors of all time and there is priceless wisdom in his proclamations.

*** Bernie Madoff owned and managed Madoff Securities. This was a trading firm on Wall Street. Now convicted felon Bernie Madoff, his brother and his two sons operated Madoff Securities. They ran an estimated $60 billion Ponzi scheme at the time of their downfall in late 2008. Investors suffered massive losses when this scheme was uncovered.

Advisor #3

1. What type of advisor are you looking for?
   - Financial planner for cash flow management and asset allocation
   - Full service advisor like a family office for more complex matters
   - Investment manager who can provide advice on securities or funds to meet a pre-determined allocation
2. What is the experience level of the advisor? It has been tough to be a new financial advisor over the past ten years. They have no claim to experience in a bear market and a very muted economic cycle. I think a "been there, seen that" advisor is invaluable during down times.
3. How are they to be paid: Product commission, retainer or fees as a percentage of assets managed? The fee-based advisors have been evolving rapidly over the last decade.
4. What is their firm like? What is the range of experience, areas of expertise and time in business? What about turnover in both professional and administrative staff and clients?
5. What about the "fit" between advisor and client? Are they both on the same wavelength? Do their personalities mesh?

As you can see, there is some overlap among these three financial advisors. There are also some special gems of advice unique to each. The point of sharing with you these three advisors opinions about how to select a financial advisor is to give you the information to help you make your best judgment in making this important decision.

Another way to find a financial advisor in your area is to go to www. napfa.org. This is the web site for The National Association of Personal Financial Advisors. Pick several and set up interview schedules. Ask all of your questions, see how the chemistry feels between the two of you and ask for references as part of the interview process. Do your due diligence and then make a selection.

Another source to locate advisors in your area is the Garrett Planning Network. Their web site is www.garrettplanningnetwork.com. This is a nationwide independent network with hundreds of fee-only financial planners. Follow the same due diligence process.

Questions to Ask a Financial Advisor

1. What is your investment philosophy and style? Are you an individual stock and bond picker, a ETFs only manager, mutual funds, manager of manager, or what?
2. What is your fee structure? Do you have different levels of fees for assets under management (AUM)? What are the fee ranges for accounts under $500,000 or up to $1.0 million or $3.0 million?
3. Are fees negotiable? Any discounts available?
4. Will I have a dedicated advisor year in and year out or do I get assigned to different people over time?
5. What services am I actually getting for my fees? Do I need all of these services?
6. What is the level of experience of the firm and my advisor? How long has my advisor been in business?
7. How often will we have a formal review of my account?
8. How will I track your performance? What is the definition of success in your advisory capacity?
9. Give me a list of references and their contact information.

One alternative option to consider rather than engaging a financial advisor for his/her full range of services is to ask an advisor for an annual check-up only. Some advisors may be willing to work with you on this basis in the short-term to help you structure your investments in the most efficient manner.

If you have concerns about making a major mistake with any of your personal investment decisions, working with a professional advisor can give you the peace of mind you need to protect your retirement nest egg. In this regard their service can be priceless!

One of my best friends is a very savvy, intelligent investor. He studies the market, analyzes economic trends and works on his portfolio every week. He is very capable of being a successful D-I-Y investor. His preference is to engage a financial advisor rather than manage on his own. When I asked him why he preferred to work with an advisor, his answer surprised me. He said, "I want to avoid the costly mistakes so many families and individuals make in managing their investments. I want multiple ideas rather than just my own. I also want to stay current with changes that affect our estate plan. It is well worth the fee." That sums up why you might consider working with a financial advisor.

Who would not like a coach or trusted professional advisor to offer guidance in helping to keep you on track to meet your investment goals? Partnering with a financial advisor can help you navigate the complexities of retirement planning. Working with a financial professional may mean the difference between a successful retirement and one filled with anxiety and uncertainty.

You are now operating from a proven, solid platform using the acquired saving and investing habit. You are well on your way to building wealth with purpose.

14

W-I-I-F-M

W-I-I-F-M. What's In It For Me? Every self-help, personal improvement, motivational and financial advice book should have a simple take-away, one that is easy to remember long after you have read the book. Here is the take-away from *Investing 1.0.1 With Purpose* that answers the question, "What's In It For Me?'

Investing for the future is not complicated. Successful wealth building is within your ability and time frame. Follow the KIS principle: Keep It Simple. A financially secure retirement is possible.

You can do this IF you make it a priority and commit to live your investing purpose with each of your daily decisions. Your changed financial behavior should reflect this investment purpose.

W-I-I-F-M

- Keep It Simple (KIS)
- Maintain Financial Discipline
- Stay Fully Invested
- Change Behavior for the Better

Why read a book or complete a course of study if there is no lasting impact on your life? If it does not change your behavior for the better, why spend the time? Every instance when you invest time and energy in learning about how to improve your life needs a BIG takeaway. That is what W-I-I-F-M is all about. W-I-I-F-M is about your future financial behavior.

Think about W-I-I-F-M takeaways from this book as important and as simple as the following:

- Turn despair into hope for the future.
- Self-realization you are not alone in the situation of not understanding the investment markets or processes. You have the power to build a new future.
- This book is intended to give you one road map to help you conquer your fears about investing. There are many others. This is only one resource.
- This book presents various model portfolio examples to help you achieve a comfortable retirement.
- To gain the self-confidence to overcome inertia that has been holding you back from achieving your retirement planning and funding goals. A call to action!
- To give you a way to automate the investment process as if operating on an autopilot.
- To gain the satisfaction that you have provided for your financial future and will not become dependent on others.
- *Investing 1.0.1 with Purpose* is not common, everyday knowledge or you would already be doing the things outlined within these chapters. If everyone were following these strategies, we would not have a looming retirement crisis.

These are all important W-I-I-F-M takeaways to help increase your personal self-esteem, as well as to change your financial behavior for the better. After all, everyone enjoys the accomplishment of being successful.

What is your definition of retirement? How close to this fantasy do you think your financial resources will allow you to live your vision of a financially secure retirement? These are important questions as you consider your many options for building wealth for the future.

Some professional advisors counsel their clients to maintain focus on only three (3) essential factors for investing success.

Three Essential Investment Success Factors

- Fees
- Taxes
- Improved Financial Behavior

We have discussed these in previous chapters but it may serve us well to review them in some more detail. Fees and taxes added together can negate your positive financial behavior.

Fees

Fees do matter! If anyone tells you they don't, **run, not walk away.** Investment returns are lowered by the amount of fees paid for investment services. Looking for the low cost provider makes sense. Passive index/ETF investing offers some of the lowest expense ratios available.

Some fees may be charged per transaction while others may be charged on the basis of assets under management (AUM). If you are being charged fees per transaction, keep the number of transactions to a minimum. There is no need to become a day trader. The lower the transaction number the lower the total cost in this example. Be sure all fees are monitored closely to avoid over paying. Your future retirement funds depend on this basic due diligence exercise. Lower fees equal more money to invest. Remember, avoid costs that do not deliver benefits. Understand what services you receive for the fees paid.

Taxes

Taxes also reduce the amount of money available for investment and can be thought of as another form of expense ultimately affecting your investment returns. Maximizing tax-deferred investments always makes the best use of scarce investment dollars. After you have contributed the maximum allowed to these tax preference accounts (IRAs and 401(k) accounts, continue investing in taxable accounts. Most active trading should be confined to the tax-deferred accounts. Taxes can arise in a taxable account when sales of securities occur and dividends and interest are earned. These taxes will eat away at your total returns.

Financial Behavior

This is the 800-pound gorilla in the room. Financial behavior includes everything from maintaining financial discipline to dollar cost averaging to automating the investment process to avoiding the common mistakes outlined in Chapter 11.

Another words, it is everything you do that affects your investment process. Emotion driven investment decisions can be one of the largest negative drags on overall returns. Avoid knee jerk reactions like selling on the day the market drops 500 points. Investment decisions based on facts, not emotions, are better for your returns.

Focus on what you can control. Make the big decisions regarding asset allocation and diversification, for example, and avoid frequent trading activity.

Be smart, be diligent and make good, fact-based decisions along the road to wealth building for the future. You will be fine, if you do.

In the next two chapters I will introduce a lower risk investment strategy that is a robust, yet non-emotional methodology to assist you in helping yourself improve your investment performance.

15

THE POWER OF IDEAS

According to Charles Darwin "It is not the strongest of the species that survive, nor the most intelligent, but the ones most responsive to change."

> Your mind is a garden,
> Your thoughts are the seeds.
> You can grow flowers or
> You can grow weeds.
> Don't forget to water it!
>
> ----Anonymous---

Ideas can be like seeds. They can grow anywhere if they are nurtured and allowed to grow without restrictions. Keeping an open mind will let new ideas flourish. We need to be responsive to change for the long-term health of our retirement accounts. Try becoming a change agent rather than resisting changes that, ultimately, are inevitable.

I encourage you to welcome change and embrace it. Stop fighting change! Life is smoother this way than fighting every change that comes along. Many of us have been raised by parents telling us to take the practical approach to life, business and investing. Too much emphasis on the practical side can cause creativity and new ideas to be frowned upon. Of course, a total disregard for the practical approach needs to have some limits, as well. Empower yourself and others to test your boundaries and overcome fear of the unknown and the untried. "This is the way we have always done it" is the epitome of fighting change and being closed minded.

As we all know, ideas are what change the world. Nothing is static and nothing can be assumed to never change or forever be the same. Be aware of what is happening around you; watch the news, talk with your contemporaries and financial professionals about how to flow with the changes that inevitably shape our world. Do not put your investment plan into hibernation or isolation; it needs to be a dynamic plan, changing when needed. It is like tending your garden. What does not change is your financial discipline to continue to fund your plan, as it may change from time to time, to meet your ultimate objectives.

Every day we read about big ideas that are changing the relationship between how we live, work and how we interact together. Think WeWork, Airbnb, Uber, Web MD, Google Search, Zillow, Taskrabbit, Lyft or VRBO, to name a few. None of these newer ideas that have the potential to change how we perform everyday tasks were around a few years ago. There is more change to come, I would bet on it and you should count on it.

Transformative ideas literally do change the world. Stay attuned to these changes by reading publications like the Wall Street Journal regularly and other financial publications. CNBC and other business TV talk shows cover a vast array of financial news daily. The power of ideas is truly amazing, for something as weightless as an idea, they can carry quite a punch.

The same is true with investing and wealth building. On-line access through the Internet has opened the world to a plethora of new ideas. Ideas are terrific but unless we take action on some of these ideas, they will just remain an idea. Probably an idea someone else will use to his or her advantage. What are you waiting for?

"Guided by the belief that good is the opposite of bad, mankind has for centuries pursued its fixation with fault and failing. Doctors have studied disease in order to learn about health. Psychologists have investigated sadness in order to learn about joy. Therapists have looked into the causes of divorce in order to learn about happy marriage. And in schools and workplaces around the world, each one of us has been encouraged to identify, analyze, and correct our weaknesses in order to become strong.

This advice is well intended but misguided. Faults and failings deserve study, but they reveal little about strengths. Strengths have their own patterns."[14]

Most of us lack understanding about our individual strengths and how to mold our future around them. You have the moral and intellectual strength to build wealth for the future. Follow the guidelines of *Investing 1.0.1 with Purpose* and help turn your talents into strengths that will produce a comfortable retirement.

At the risk of repeating myself, these pre-qualifiers for investing are so important that I will repeat them again. You must have provided for these seven (7) financial priorities before you start to invest: health insurance, disability insurance, life insurance, an emergency cash account, 401(k) participation, IRA and savings. Each of these priorities mitigates a risk that could impair your ability to invest for the long-term, if they have not been properly covered. This is the essence of my financial wellness agenda.

It is time for a reality check along with a cautionary note. After eight years of good returns in the stock market ending 12-31-2017, investors have become accustomed to ever rising markets. At the same time, cautious investors should have some concern that the market may suffer exhaustion or severe fatigue at some point. No one knows when the market may become too over valued but you should stay alert to the signs of a turn from bullish to bearish moves in the markets (bullish is positive and bearish is negative). It always pays to be mindful that markets inevitably correct. Nothing goes up forever!

There is occasionally some talk of a pending asset bubble. I do not know if the current market is, in fact, in some type of bubble, but I do recognize there are increasing signs of euphoria and irrational behavior with regard to the stock market. Valuations seem high, but are they too high? No one knows for sure.

What do I mean by an asset bubble? It is a type of economic event when market investors drive stock prices above their real or rational values. It can be associated with groupthink and herd behavior. Bubbles can occur in a specific market sector like technology or in multiple sectors at the same time like housing and financial sectors. Asset bubbles are usually sector specific, not market wide. Bubbles can become speculative in nature that lead to panic selling and sudden decreases in prices.

---

[14] *NOW, DISCOVER YOUR STRENGTHS,* by Marcus Buckingham and Donald O. Clifton, Ph.D., THE FREE PRESS, 2001, p 3

If an asset bubble does develop, then investors will have a chance to make money, lose money or to miss out and pass on participating in the event entirely. I want you to have some choices with how you may respond, if there is a significant market pullback caused by the bursting of an asset bubble or an overall market correction.

Stocks, like everything else, will not go up in value in a continuous straight line. They will adjust when they become too expensive and are out of sync with the values of their underlying companies. When stock prices spiral downward there will be buying opportunities. This is called buying on the dips in the market.

Look for buying opportunities on the dip. Buying on the dips is one of my core trading strategies to take advantage of market volatility. I call this rebalancing driven by opportunity. If your time horizon is long enough (10-15-20 years), staying fully invested has been the winning strategy. Panic selling is always a bad move.

What is the difference between an asset bubble and a market correction? I have already shared with you my definition of an asset bubble. A market correction may affect the whole market. It is a reverse movement (usually always falling) in price of at least 10% in the total market value of all stocks, ETFs or indexes. It occurs to adjust for the over valuation of these assets. The good news is that market corrections are usually temporary and a recovery typically occurs within a few months.

If I have frightened you with this dose of reality or if you are overly concerned about a major market correction, there are at least four options you might consider.

Options to Consider if Worried About a Market Correction

1. Go to cash now or bank FDIC insured products
2. Sell at the first sign of a correction
3. Stay the course
4. Shift asset allocations more toward international stocks or bonds

Cash

We talked about the risks of going to cash and getting out of the market in Chapter 11. The key concern here is getting out of the market too early and getting back in too late. Who has a crystal ball that is clear enough to avoid this risk? Cash has a low rate of return even when invested in bank insured deposits. Not a good move for everyday investors.

Sell at the first sign of a correction

Here the question is what is the right timing for such a move? Who thinks they are smart enough to be able to call a market correction before it starts or exactly when it starts? I do not know of any financial analyst that is this good. Do you? Probably not a good choice.

Stay the course

This is a default option. Afraid to exercise any of the other options, this is the only remaining one that might make sense. Time in the market has proven to be an antidote for overcoming market corrections. It takes nerves of steel and fortitude to withstand the short-term pain caused by a severe correction. This would be my recommended option for everyday investors.

Shift asset allocations toward international stocks or bonds

This is not a perfect solution either. A market correction in the US stock market may also pull down the values of international stocks as many investors may withdraw from the market in total. International stocks and emerging markets stocks might recover faster, but it is no guarantee.

Bond prices may also be affected in a correction. The good news about bonds is the steady and reliable interest payments they provide. At least your cash flow can be maintained with these high quality, investment grade assets.

The choice among and between any of these options is always yours. Do what makes you feel comfortable but make your choice on the basis of factual data, not emotional, gut wrenching fear or following the herd mentality. Remember, when others are rushing for the market exits, good buying opportunities are available.

If you are committed to a strategy of long-term investing, short-term fluctuations in market values are of less concern. Just do not become a greedy buyer in these uncertain times. Cautious optimism is always the best approach. Bubbles and market corrections are all about survival as an investor. The future of the world's economy still appears to be positive and worthy of continued long-term investment.

What is the difference between corrections, recessions and stock market crashes? These terms are **not** interchangeable.

Corrections are considered common events and I have defined them above. They have occurred once a year, on average.

Recessions are an economic term that refers to a general drop in economic activity over two (2) or more consecutive quarters. While a recession may cause the stock market to decline, the term recession is not a specific stock market event. Recessions occur on average every 3-5 years.

A stock market crash is the most severe of these terms. It is a rapid drop in all stock prices. The Crash of 1929 is a good example of a market crash. These crashes are considered very unusual events, causing panic selling.

The bottom line is the market has always recovered from any and all of these events. The only question is, how long will it take to recover the next time? The committed long-term investor has one of the best opportunities to survive these jolting events. History is on the side of the long-term investor!

Human behavior is always a fascinating subject and topic to study. I have tried to learn about human behavior from my own experiences, as well as observing others. I ask people all the time why they made certain investment decisions and I am amazed by the lack of thoughtfulness some people put into their decision-making.

Some of the reasons given by my seminar participants overtime regarding why they bought a particular stock have included the following:

- I like the company's advertising as seen on TV (Risk: advertising and investment performance are not directly related)
- I use their products and I like how they work (Risk: What about competition, sustainability and profitability?)
- I am an employee of this company and I like buying my employer's stock (Risk: Watch buying too much stock in the company where

you work, as you also earn your living from the same company. Avoid a concentration in your company's stock)

- My friend recommended this company because he/she knows their CEO or CFO (Risk: Knowing senior management is nice but not a good reason to buy the stock. A better thing to know is the company's performance matrixes.)

I have highlighted some high risks for investors in each instance, notwithstanding the fact these were reasons for buying an individual stock. I am not recommending individual stocks for everyday investors.

History can also be a teacher from whom we can learn about human nature.

Historical amnesia, however, leaves us doomed to repeat mistakes from the past. The only antidote is to remember accurately what actually happened in the past and try to avoid doing the same thing over and over with an expectation of a different outcome. Is this not the definition of insanity?

If I were to compile a checklist of ideas that should contribute toward making a positive difference in helping everyday investors be successful in wealth building, it would include at least these twenty (20) action steps.

Checklist of Ideas for Success

1. Learn to live below your means at an early age and stay with this plan throughout your life.
2. Save early and often! When it comes to saving a portion of your gross income, think in terms of saving a percentage of your gross income rather than a specific dollar amount.
3. Learn to budget early in your career as a way to understand where you are spending money and where to focus your attention in making some changes in your spending patterns.
4. Learn to spend smarter and better not just stop spending. If you think about the difference between "needs to have" versus "wants to have" when it comes to spending, you will spend in a more deliberate manner.
5. Diversification is an important concept in the investment process. With investments it means spreading your dollars among different asset classes like stocks, bonds, real estate and broad market indexes.

It also should mean to invest in both tax-advantaged accounts (IRA and 401(k) accounts) as well as taxable accounts. The taxable accounts should provide more of the rocket fuel for growth in your portfolio.

6. Another concept of applying diversification might be to develop multiple sources of income while living in retirement. These may include a part-time job, a hobby that becomes a source of income, investments in rental income real estate, consulting or selling garage sale items on eBay, to name a few examples.

7. Asset allocation is the process of dividing your investment dollars among the various asset classes. Asset allocation is one way to achieve diversification. Allocating different percentages among the various assets will have an impact on your long-term returns. Asset allocation drives returns.

8. Rebalance your portfolio annually or when opportunity presents itself.

9. Working with a financial advisor (RIA) can help keep you on track to achieve your wealth building goals. A fee only financial advisor can fill the role of coach, trusted financial advisor, guidance counselor and best friend. Who else are you comfortable sharing all of your financial information with along with your future hopes and dreams?

10. Keep It Simple (KIS). This is my recurring theme. The path to success in wealth building does not need to be complicated. Only individuals make it complicated. Avoid over complicating the wealth building process. Follow the KIS Principle.

11. Taking action is essential to turning possibilities into progress. Otherwise, it is only a passing thought. Take advantage of financial opportunities when they occur. Do not wait for a better opportunity to come along later.

12. Keep your focus on long-term investment returns and accept that short and mid-term risks are unavoidable. Stay focused on the things you can control.

13. Costs do matter. Keep all investment costs as low as possible. The lower the expense ratio the better. Fees, taxes and any other investment expense eat into your future returns.

14. Passive investing is as dull as dishwater but it offers the highest probability of long-term investment success for everyday investors.

15. The old rule of 100 minus your age should be the percentage (%) of your portfolio held in stocks is a good starting point for asset allocation. Vary this percentage and you are at peril for significant negative consequences for the long-term value of your total portfolio. (Example: 100 – 67 (FRA)= 33% held in stocks). This is an ultraconservative formula. Asset allocation does affect the total return on your portfolio. Understanding your personal risk tolerance will help you chose an asset allocation with which you can be comfortable.

16. When the stock market declines, do not sell. Look for buying opportunities. Big dips in the market are big opportunities. Stay fully invested. Time in the market should enhance your total returns.

17. Remember to apply the Rule of 72 to help monitor your progress and help keep you on track to achieve your investment purpose. If the time required to double your investment is beyond your time horizon, you should become more aggressive with choosing higher yielding investments.

18. Avoid the Dirty Dozen Plus One mistakes that can drain your retirement accounts prematurely discussed in Chapter 10.

19. Avoid the common investment mistakes highlighted in Chapter 11.

20. Be a change agent and keep your mind open to new ideas. The one guarantee you can count on is that things will change over your investment horizon.

With these new investment perspectives and ideas, how do you bring it all together and put it into a plan of action? This is the topic of the last chapter.

16

RECIPE FOR SUCCESS

OR

"A GOLDILOCKS PLAN"

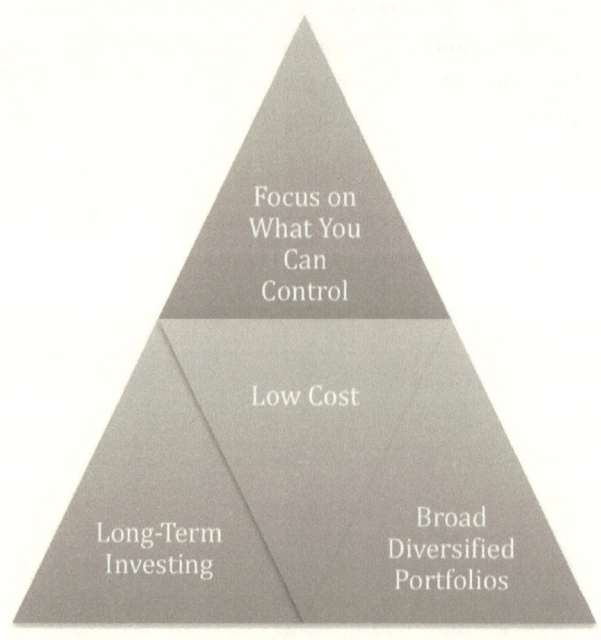

Who can resist a grand plan enumerated with the boundless promise of a better tomorrow? This is exactly what you get with *Investing 1.0.1 with Purpose.*

I promised to highlight a lower risk investment strategy that will allow you to achieve your financial goals and also let you sleep well at night, without fear and anxiety about the daily performance of the stock market. This strategy for a better financial future is what I call my Recipe for Success, or "A Goldilocks Plan". It is not too hot or too cold; it is just the right temperature. This plan may be just right for you.

The pyramid summarizes in four sections the essence of my investing recommendations. It is a simple yet eloquent graphic illustration of the successful components of my recipe for success. It may need some explaining to convince you that investing for future wealth building can be boiled down to this simplistic pyramid. The "Goldilocks Plan" is singularly focused on structuring your investment accounts to be" just right" for you. The components of the plan involve a long-term investing approach, low costs, a broad, diversified portfolio, while all along focusing on what you can control.

Long Term Investing

Long-term investors have a time horizon of 10-20 years or longer. They are not distracted from their investment objectives by short-term fluctuations in the markets. They recognize that perfection in investing is never attainable. There are too many variables that influence the price or market value of various stocks and bonds. The best you can do as an everyday investor is to minimize mistakes.

Low Cost

Costs do matter! The fees paid and any taxes due, as a result of selling a security, reduce the total return on a stock or bond portfolio. In 20 years, a 1.0% annual fee can reduce portfolio values by nearly $30,000, compared to a portfolio with a 0.25% annual fee, by my estimate. Keep expense ratios (fees) as low as practical and look for tax efficiency within any fund.

Diversified Portfolios

In investing, just as in life, there are few certainties you can count on. Essentially, this concept refers to spreading your investments among different asset classes to mitigate risk and increase the total return of your portfolio. Asset classes, for example, might include US stocks of large, medium and small sized companies, as well as international stocks, bonds and perhaps real estate. After diversification comes asset allocation, or the percentage invested in each asset class.

Focus on What You Can Control

This is pretty straightforward. Do you spend time worrying about the weather? Do you agonize over the next disaster to occur, either man made or Mother Nature driven? Are you obsessed with how your cell phone works? I hope the answer to these questions is a resounding NO! All three of these are not within your control. When it comes to investing for the long-term, focus on those things fully in your control like:

1. When to start investing
2. How much to invest
3. How often to invest
4. What asset classes to invest in (both diversification and allocation)
5. Maintain your financial discipline by automating the investment process
6. Live below your means
7. Make rational decisions rather than being driven by emotions
8. Make the habit of saving and investing part of your daily life

When you successfully live by the four components of "A Goldilocks Plan" the results should lead to achieving a higher level of financial success. There are as many definitions of financial success as there are individual investors. The definition is very personal. For me, financial success is the freedom that you achieve with realizing your financial goals, whatever they are. Freedom to do what you want, when you want and with whomever. This definition can also be your financial wellness criteria. Financial success is a direct result of your change in financial behavior. This is a result of taking charge of your personal wealth building for the future.

When you cut through all the noise and hype from Wall Street, the real success on Main Street for all everyday investors can be measured by market returns, an acceptable level of investment risk and the resulting, low amount of personal stress created from the investment process. The pyramid highlighting my recipe for success delivers all three of these success factors, in spades.

Let's look at the "Goldilocks Plan" in another way. Some people prefer to see important information outlined in a table. I believe this investment recommendation is so important, I want to repeat it in this different format:

A Goldilocks Plan in Table Format

Components	Reasoning
Long-term investing	Stay fully invested; do not worry about short-term fluctuations in the values of your portfolios; maintain financial discipline; automate the investment process;
Low cost	Fees and expenses reduce performance; seek out low expense ratios and tax efficiency
Diversified portfolios	Diversification in asset categories, reasonable mix of stocks and bonds and a combination of domestic and international exposure
Focus on what you can control	Adapt to the investment process and keep your end goal in sight. Pay particular attention to the things that matter most like getting started early with saving and investing, maintaining financial discipline throughout your life and making rational decisions

I would add one additional component critical to the success of the compounding benefits of successful investing. A focus on tax efficiency is a very important consideration. The tax drag associated with taxable accounts lowers their overall performance numbers. Continuing to hold investments in tax-advantaged accounts like IRAs and 401 (k) plans can neutralize some of this negative drag. At the end of the day, what matters most is what you keep, after taxes.

Additional Component

Tax Efficiency	It is not how much money you have, what matters most is what you keep, after taxes

Earlier in this book, I discussed the high level of complexity involved with many investment strategies. I may error too far on the other side by over simplifying but I am convinced there is a lack of adequate, plain vanilla advice offered to everyday investors. This is exactly what they seek. It is like asking a surgeon about your last operation. All you want to know, as the patient is, "was the operation successful?" You do not want the details about the incision, how long you were on the operating table, which organs had to be relocated during surgery, the number of pints of blood transfused and the myriad of specialists called in to consult. That is too much information.

This is why I am such a proponent of The KIS Principle (Keep It Simple). If an investment strategy cannot be explained in plain language on one sheet of 8 ½ x 11 piece of paper, then it may be too complex for a lot of people. When a subject is too complicated, people either tune out, take no action or they may blindly put all their trust in a financial professional to execute on the complicated strategy. I do not think this is the way it should be.

It has been said that any fierce debate often generates more friction than enlightenment. This may be the case in the on-going face-off between the sharply divided advocates of passive versus actively managed investment accounts. My purpose in writing on the subject of investing has been to take the mystery out of investing for everyday investors Passive investing through an index fund and/or ETFs can and should be a starting point. It can also remain the appropriate strategy for the rest of your life. There may be a need to modify some of the allocations between stocks and bonds as you age but the passive indexing strategy should deliver on the promise of long-term wealth building.

On the cost side of investing, why should anyone believe that a higher cost results in better performance? I have not seen any studies that can validate such a theory. In fact most of the studies I have read indicate the opposite is true. Lower cost structures can and do provide good value and better, long-term investment performance. Remember, the important number is what you keep after taxes and expenses.

I have highlighted some of the many risks involved with investing in the markets. Phrases like "Prior performance does not guarantee future results" are commonplace within investment literature. Almost all market investments lack FDIC insurance and the risk of losing money is always possible in any transaction. No one should believe there is any magic "silver bullet" when it comes to investing.

Two specific individual mistakes I have seen wreck havoc with retirees investment accounts have been investing too aggressively and over spending in the early years of retirement. Avoid these mistakes and do not allow these two actions to destroy your retirement plans.

- **Investing too aggressively.** If you have struggled throughout your career to adequately fund your retirement accounts, do not assume you can make it up in retirement through aggressive investing. Once retired, the time for taking excess investment risk has passed. High risk investing is for the young, if there is any justification for high risk, because the young investor has time to recover from any mistakes. In retirement you do not have time on your side. When you ignore your asset allocation methodology, you are adding unnecessary risk. Investing is always about maintaining a good balance between risk and reward.
- **Over spending in the early years of retirement.** After retirement, you have time and money at your disposal, if you have planned well earlier in your career. The temptation to spend money on travel, bigger toys like a new boat, recreational vehicle (RV), motorcycle or other big-ticket items can be overwhelming. It may be appropriate to spend money on these things but you must exercise some discipline to avoid spending too much. The number ONE thing you are seeking in retirement is to NEVER run out of money and become financially dependent on others. If you want your retirement funds to last for the duration of you and your spouses golden years, then

sticking with your withdrawal rate is very important. Remember the rule of thumb of withdrawing no more than 4% of your fund balance annually? No retiree should ever be unhappy if you have some leftover funds in your retirement accounts after you depart this world.

Fixed income investing (bonds and bond funds) is of interest to everyday investors because bonds offer additional diversity, lower volatility and income in the form of semi-annual interest payments. However, there are three primary risks for the debt holder of bonds:

- Fixed income investing includes interest rate risk. Typically, when interest rates rise, there is a corresponding decline in bond values or prices. The interest rate paid by a bond is fixed. (There are some variable rate bonds on the market but I am not recommending them.) If you hold a bond to maturity, you will be paid the face amount of the bond. In a rising rate environment, alternative bond investments will be offering higher interest rates than a pool of bonds of like quality purchased years ago.
- Fixed income investing also includes credit risks. This refers to the possibility that the bond issuer will not be able to make principal and interest payments when due for financial reasons, such as a default or restructure.
- Loss of purchasing power is a real risk with bonds. As inflation increases, the purchasing power of a fixed income investment decreases. Keeping maturities in the 3-5 year range may help mitigate some of this risk.
- Remember to include your social security benefits as part of your fixed income allocation. While the annual benefits may be adjusted by changes in the cost of living (COLA), this government annuity is intended to provide funds for your entire lifetime.

Index funds and ETFs have demonstrated they are simple to understand and explain while also more predictable, if anything about the market is predictable. They are predictable in the sense they should deliver a market rate of return, close to the return of their specific index.

These two qualities of index funds and ETFs should not be dismissed, or diminished.

This is not to say either of these is future-proof. There are no guarantees in the stock market.

Index funds have outperformed more than two-thirds of actively managed funds across all types of markets. They have been dependable performers achieving at or near their index performance numbers for decades. I have no reason to think they will not continue to achieve their index average. They just plod along doing their job without fanfare.

For the full year of 2017, the overall total return by separate asset class was impressive. Here are three (3) major asset class performance numbers.

2017 Total Return
According to Thomson Re0uters Lipper Data

- US Stocks 18.3%
- International
- Stocks 26.8%
- Intermediate

Bonds 3.6%

While these total returns are very good, do they really matter? Not so much, when you are a committed long-term investor. I prefer to stay focused on the 3-5 and 10-year performance numbers as a better gauge of longer-term performance.

I highlight the latest annual market performance numbers to reinforce my argument favoring the wealth building power of the stock and bond markets. My personal experience has shown wealth building can be as straight forward as a five-legged stool consisting of real estate, a mix of stocks, ETFs and bonds, home ownership, retirement accounts like 401(k) accounts and IRAs and living debt free. You can construct your own plan with as many legs to the stool as you want.

After all the discussion about the investment process, its background, fundamentals and conquering life's bigger financial issues, what would a plain vanilla investment strategy look like? If I were trying to model a plan for your consideration, a model portfolio for everyday investors might include the following three (3) index/ETF funds. These would become my core holdings.

MODEL PORTFOLIO FOR EVERYDAY INVESTORS

CORE HOLDINGS

1. Vanguard Total Stock Market Index (VTSAX or VTI for the ETF) **ADMIRAL SHARES**

   This fund will give you exposure to the total US stock market, which will include large, midcap and small cap companies. **The expense ratio is 0.04%.** This fund tracks the CRSP US Total Market Index, which includes approximately 3,800 companies. The average return over the past 5 years has been 15.55%. The minimum investment in Admiral shares is $10,000.

   Allocate 60%

2. Vanguard FTSE All-World Index (VFWAX or VEU for the ETF)

   This fund tracks the FTSE All-World ex-US Index by investing in approximately 2,200 companies representing 44 countries (non USA). Approximately 43% of the fund is invested in European companies, 30% in the Pacific region, 21% in emerging markets and 6% in North American firms (Canada). As some of this fund's assets are invested in emerging markets, I see no need for a separate fund for that category. The average return over the past 5 years has been 7.44 %. **The expense ratio is 0.11%.**

   Allocate 15%

3. Vanguard Intermediate-Term Corporate Bond Fund (VICSX or VCIT for the ETF)

   I prefer this corporate bond fund to the total bond market because the total market fund holds a number of Treasury Bonds. The Treasury bonds add additional safety but lower the yield. The Intermediate-term corporate bond fund tracks the Barclays Capital

US 5-10 Year Corporate Bond Index, with an average credit rating of triple B (investment grade). This fund has an average return of 3.42 % over the past 5 years. **The expense ratio is 0.07%.**

Allocate 25%

Source: Vanguard[15]

The Goldilocks Plan

In Action

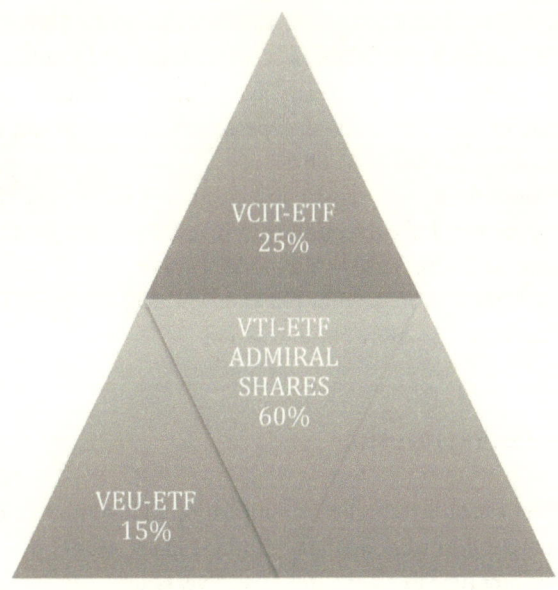

---

[15] These 5 Vanguard Index Funds Are All You Need, by Stephen Goldberg, Kiplinger Newsletter, 2015, http://amp.kiplinger.com/article/investing.com

As you can see, I have a preference for the Vanguard Group of funds. Vanguard invented the concept of index funds and has continually lowered the cost of these funds offered to the public. They are not always the highest performing, but they deliver good value for the price. I also like the Admiral shares of the Vanguard Funds and the symbols above are those of the Admiral shares for each index. This class of shares has a minimum investment of $10,000.00 versus $3,000.00 minimum in the regular Vanguard funds. The Admiral shares typically have a lower expense ratio than the regular shares. Remember, costs matter when it comes to the total return numbers.

I have not included the Standard & Poor's 500 stock index fund in this model portfolio recommendation. The S&P 500 index began in 1957 and has a reliable, long-term performance record. There is nothing wrong with including this index. It is a very good index for tracking the performance of large cap US companies. It is limited by this focus on large cap stocks only. It is not as broad or complete a portfolio as represented by my three recommendations above. If you have a preference for the S&P 500 Index, then include it in your portfolio mix as a core holding. I would not object, although my preference would be the equivalent ETF index whose symbol is SPDR S&P 500(SPY). SPY has an expense ratio of 0.09 % and an average return over the past 5 years of 15.68 %.

The expense ratios and five-year average returns are all as of 12-31-2017.

Now you see why I like the minimalist investment strategy of only using 3-4 funds and/or ETFs. VEU – VTI – VCIT and SPY, if you choose to include it, makeup my core holdings in an investment portfolio. This is one example of Less-Can-Be-More put into action.

Become a boring investor

I have shared with you a lot of information. This information is only helpful if you put it to work and take action. I knew a CEO who was fond of saying "the best time to plant a tree was 25 years ago." My own additional follow-on statement is "The second best time is today!" What this translates to in our context is the overwhelming need to take some investment action now and avoid drifting along with the current of everyday life. This is the only way I know to build a nest egg to be enjoyed at full retirement age (FRA) and beyond.

Designing your investment portfolio should be centered on boring, stable, low-volatility stocks. History has shown these types of investments, as represented by the index funds/ETFs I have recommended, have outperformed actively managed accounts over time. Become a boring investor. Invest in a broadly diversified portfolio of low fee index and ETF funds that track broad market indices.

My final test for determining the level of appropriateness for any investment recommendation is what I call the Rip Van Winkle test. Assume you fall asleep and stay asleep for 20 years. Or assume you enter a medically induced coma and wake up 20 years later. The concept is the same. Will your retirement investment plan continue to have performed well or will it have fallen off track for the lack of your attention?

If your plan relies on your active and frequent input to stay current with the market, then I believe, as an everyday investor, you have the wrong plan. On the other hand, if your plan will continue to perform by matching market returns year in and year out without your input over those 20 years you are not available, then I think it is the right plan for you. The Goldilocks Plan passes my Rip Van Winkle test with a grade of A++!

Indexing and exchange traded funds (ETF's) have flattened and broadened the playing field for everyday investors. Today, all Americans can participate inexpensively and conveniently by investing in markets, countries and strategies once open only to institutions and large dollar investors. Consider implementing my "Goldilocks Plan." Owning broadly diversified, low cost index funds and ETFs may seem as exciting as watching grass grow. After you make an investment, the funds should grow in close alignment with the market indexes you have chosen. These core investments can last a lifetime.

You can borrow aspects from any of these formats to sync up with the rhythms of your contemporary life. Ultimately, any "Goldilocks Plan" you chose should be one that works best for you and your family. I think of "The Goldilocks Plan" like a "code of the road." Breathe life into this plan by living by this "code of the road."

"Code of the road" is a phrase supporting a few basic rules to live by while traveling the road to building wealth for the future. "The Goldilocks Plan" is the essence or map for the code.

My hope is that you live a long, productive life, culminating in good health, the shared love of a spouse and family and the financial security of a well planned, well executed wealth building strategy, along with the time to enjoy all of them.

While the future may appear uncertain, I have always believed strongly in a person's ability to shape their future. Human beings are the only species who can determine their personal future, subject to maintaining good health. Taking action to control your future is so much more rewarding than being controlled by life's ebb and flow of unrelated circumstances. I still believe "our best years are ahead of us!" Follow the theme of *Investing 1.0.1 with Purpose* and make it a part of your daily activities.

You are ready to begin the wealth-building journey on your own. Taking on the challenges of various short-term risks to obtain long-term growth opportunities available through stock ownership can be exhilarating. Stay calm, make rational decisions, develop financial discipline and enjoy the journey. Make the "Goldilocks Plan" a part of the predictable rhythm of your life.

As you have now become an equity investor, put the wind at your back and let the growing economy of the USA and the developed world propel you forward to achieve your financial goals. You will be glad you did!

Investing 1.0.1 with Purpose ends at the moment your future begins. Make the most of it

CONSERVATIVE PORTFOLIO EXAMPLES

AGE 30-50

Stock	Fixed Income
90% With 70% domestic stock (VTI) and 20% international equities (VEU). If you are going to take investment risks, this is the time.	10% Short to intermediate bonds with maximum maturities 5-7 years. Include only corporate bonds. (VCIT)

AGE 50-67

Stock	Fixed Income
80% With 60% domestic stock (VTI) and 20% international equities (VEU). These are the high earning years to build your retirement account balances.	20% Short to intermediate bonds with maximum maturity of 5-7 years. Include a mix of corporate and US government bonds. (VCIT)

AGE 67 (FRA) AND BEYOND

Stocks	Fixed Income
70% With 60% domestic stock (VTI) and 10% international equities (VEU). Minimize investment risks at this stage of life.	30% Short to intermediate bonds with maximum maturity of 5-7 years. Include a mix of corporate and US government bonds. (VCIT)

OLD IRISH BLESSING

May the road rise up to meet you,

May the wind always be at your back.

May the sun shine warm upon your face.

An additional thought:

May your investments provide for a financially comfortable retirement.

RESOURCE LIST

Here is a list of websites and books that I have found to be
helpful for both investing and retirement planning.

Websites

Annuity Comparisons, Income Calculator is helpful comparing various
immediate annuity options; www.immediateannuities.com

The Blue Zones, life expectancy calculator; www.bluezones.com

Bogelheads, advice about investing and retirement planning from John Bogel;
www.bogelheads.com

Fidelity Retirement Income Calculator for investing; www.fidelity.com

Investing and retirement planning along with calculators; www.schwab.com

Investing and retirement planning; www.tdameritrade.com

Mutual funds and ETF investing; www.vanguard.com

T Rowe Price Retirement Calculator; www.troweprice.com

Required Minimum Distribution table and other tax questions; www.irs.gov

Social Security rules for benefits and other; www.ssa.gov

www.adviserinformation.sec.gov; due diligence and background check of potential financial advisor

www.napfa.org; a source to locate a financial advisor in your area

www.garrettplanningnetwork.com; a source to locate independent financial advisors

Books

Enough, by John C. Bogle, John Wiley & Sons, Inc, 2007

How to Make Your Money Last, by Jane Bryant Quinn, Simon & Schuster, 2016

The 5 Mistakes Every Investor Makes, by Peter Mallouk, JD, MBA, CFP, John Wiley & Sons, Inc, 2014

Money for Life, by Steve Vernon, FSA, Rest-of-Life Communications, 2012

NOW, DISCOVER YOUR STRENGTHS, by Marcus Buckingham and Donald O. Clifton, Ph.D., THE FREE PRESS, 2001

You Can Retire Sooner Than You Think, by Wes Moss, McGraw Hill Education, 2014

GLOSSARY

1. Accredited Investor – an investor whose net worth is at least $1,000,000, excluding the value of their primary residence or has income of at least $200,000 in the past two years ($300,000 if married)
2. Active Investment Management – a style of investing with a portfolio manager who makes specific investments with the goal of outperforming an investment benchmark or index
3. Annuities – an insurance contract with an insurance company that promises to pay a fixed amount of money for your life, after giving the insurance company a lump sum of money
4. Asset Allocation – an investment strategy that attempts to balance risk and reward by adjusting the percentage of each asset in the portfolio based on the investors risk profile and investment time frame
5. Autopilot – this involves the funding of investments by establishing automatic transfers on a regular basis to your selected investment accounts; It can also be the hands-off approach to investing by selecting an index fund and staying with it for the long term
6. Binary – something having two parts
7. Dollar Cost Averaging – an investing strategy that invests a fixed sum periodically overtime with the expectation to remove the impact of large purchases
8. ETF – stands for exchange traded fund and is a marketable security that tracts an index

9. Everyday Investors – this is my definition of individual investors whose training and careers are not financially oriented; this is the investor living next door as your neighbor

10. Financial Discipline – the ability to live within your pre-determined budget; a form of behavior that shows your commitment to achieve your financial goals; regular contributions are made to retirement accounts over the long term

11. Financial Literacy –the ability to use knowledge and acquired skills to manage an individuals financial responsibilities; basic financial knowledge

12. Financial Wellness – this is my definition of the understanding and ability to commit to funding the seven requirements to provide financial protection for a family; these include an emergency cash fund, health insurance, disability insurance, life insurance, 401 (k) participation, individual retirement account and creating a savings habit

13. Full Retirement Age (FRA) – Upon attaining FRA, full retirement benefits become available from Social Security; Social Security Administration has published a table showing benefits based on an individuals age; persons born 1943-1954 attain FRA at 66; those born 1960 or later FRA is age 6

14. Gig Economy – this is today's employment market; work is performed on a short-term basis or freelance, without permanent employment; benefits are limited for these independent contractors

15. Index Funds – this is a mutual fund or ETF designed to follow a specific investment benchmark or index

16. Individual Retirement Account (IRA) – a savings account designed to help individuals save for retirement; these accounts offer tax advantages; there are two types of IRA: traditional and Roth

17. Inertia – a behavior tendency to do nothing or remain unchanged

18. Investment Objective – the purpose for which an individual invests, such as retirement

19. Investment Risk – a level of uncertainty of achieving an expected return based on the individual's anticipated rate of return; all investments have risk

20. Longevity Gap – the difference between life expectancy between men and women; for my purposes, this is the difference between your actuarial life expectancy and the number of years you live

21. Passive Investment Management – an investment strategy that tracks an index or other benchmark; very little human interaction with the portfolio

22. Rainey Day Fund – a reserve of funds to be used for unexpected events such as an auto mechanical failure or emergency medical procedures

23. Rational Approach – a behavioral decision making process based on facts, not emotions

24. Rebalance – an investment process to rebalance or realign a portfolio to maintain the original asset allocation; involves buying and selling securities to achieve an original asset allocation model

25. Required Minimum Distribution (RMD) – the minimum amount you must withdraw from a traditional IRA each year; the annual RMD is set by the Internal Revenue Service; RMD must begin no later than the account holders age 70 ½; penalties for failure to withdraw the minimum annual amount are severe

26. Rule of 72 – a shortcut to estimate the number of years required to double money saved or invested at a stated annual rate of return; divide 72 by the rate

27. Vesting Schedule – in a retirement plan vesting means the percentage ownership transferred to the individual each year; 100% vesting means the individual owns the entire account balance; usually of importance where the employer match occurs

28. Wealth Effect – a change in spending that occurs with a change in perceived wealth; as an individuals residence increases in value because of market conditions, the homeowner feels more wealthy, for example

29. Withdrawal Rate – how much money an individual withdraws from their retirement accounts annually; a conservative withdrawal rate will help an individual stretch their retirement funds longer

30. 401 (k) Plan – a defined contribution plan with tax advantages for the employee making contributions as a deduction from their paycheck; employee chooses investment options from a limited menu; plan usually sponsored by the employer; may include a matching contribution from the employer; subject to Internal Revenue Service restrictions and guidelines

INDEX

NOTES

The Great Seduction

1. *Enough* by John C. Bogel, John Wiley & Sons, Inc, 2009

Chapter 2 Legend of the Gordian Knot

2. The four sources are given in Robin Lane Fox, *Alexander the Great* (1973) 1986: notes to Chapter 10, p 518; Fox recounts the anecdote, pp 149-151

Chapter 3 Why Invest

3. Enough by John C. Bogel, Wiley & Sons, Inc, 2009
4. Longevity gap is a term coined by Jane Bryant Quinn, financial journalist and a leading commentator on personal finance

Chapter 4 Choices

5. The 3 Rules to a Less Complicated Life by Lou Holtz, www.m.youtube.com

Chapter 5 Priorities

6. Individual Retirement Account Contribution Limits. www.irs.gov

Chapter 6 Debt Anchor

7. Tax Deductibility, Publication 17, Your Federal Income Tax for Individuals, and Publication 550, Investment Interest and Expenses, www.irs.gov
8. FICO Score, www.investopedia.com

Chapter 8 Investment Strategy Overload

9. 10 Long Term Investing Strategies That Work. www.investingmoney.usnews.com
10. S&P 500 Index Sectors, www.thebalance.com

Chapter 10 Solve the Retirement Conundrum

11. Fidelity Retirement Guideline, www.fidelity.com
12. Fidelity Retirement Estimator, www.fidelity.com

Chapter 13 Financial Advisors

13. Registered Investment Advisors must be registered with the federal Securities Exchange Commission or the state securities office

Chapter 15 The Power of Ideas

14. Now, Discover Your Strengths, by Marcus Buckingham and Donald O. Clifton, Ph.D., THE FREE PRESS, 2001

Chapter 16 Recipe for Success

15. These 5 Vanguard Index Funds Are All You Need, by Steven Goldberg, Kiplinger Newsletter, 2015, http://amp.kiplinger.com/article/investing

ABOUT THE AUTHOR

I have become a personal advocate for helping those who want to help themselves face the retirement challenge, head on.

We share a common goal. I receive personal satisfaction by helping others improve their financial future. You take-away information and ideas that have the potential to dramatically improve your long-term financial security. This results in a symbiotic relationship with each of us helping the other to achieve a personal goal. I hope this book will help everyday investors who want to help themselves.

I am a retired commercial banker with more than 40 years experience of working with small business owners and their families, helping them to achieve their financial objectives. I have seen many success stories over these four plus decades of hands on involvement but I have also witnessed dismal failures along the way. What separates the successes from the failures? I share some of those insights within this book.

I have no known conflicts of interest in writing this book and promoting the investment strategies outlined within this publication. I do not receive any form of compensation in the form of commissions or fees from any broker, dealer, sales organization or any other source as a result of my recommendations. I am not a securities salesperson nor am I an insurance agent.

I am a private citizen who has learned from his personal investment mistakes. I have worked the past 40 years to create an investment portfolio that delivers a comfortable retirement lifestyle for my family. By sharing these successes with you, I can help you avoid the mistakes that others and I have made on the road to wealth building.

I have owned two manufacturing/assembly companies in the office lighting and computer accessory markets. I know the challenges of meeting a payroll every week.

I founded an alternative investment fund after retiring from banking with a focus on lending to small businesses and their owner families. I am the managing partner of this fund. I work on a referral basis only, "delivering financial solutions" to our clients.

I am a published author having written two books on retirement planning. The two books are *Put Time on Your Side* and *Time to Catch Up*. Both are available from Amazon.com in either paperback or eBooks format.

I have an undergraduate degree and an MBA from the University of Missouri, with an emphasis in finance. I served more than 4 years on active duty in the US Army, as a Finance Officer and attained the rank of Captain by the time of my honorable discharge. My wife and I have three grown children of whom we are very proud. We also have four grandchildren. We reside in Overland Park, Kansas.

A special "Thank You" and heartfelt appreciation goes to my beloved wife, Coline, who has tirelessly remained patient and supportive through countless hours, days and activities related to the writing of this book. I could not have completed *Investing 1.0.1 with Purpose* without her encouragement and emotional understanding.

Together, we enjoy the measured pace of living with what retirement has to offer.

We are following the advice in this book and enjoying our retirement years. To live in Kansas is to live in what seems like another time. Traditions remain of knowing our neighbors; sitting on the front porch listening to the rhythm of the rain; working in our flower garden; and enjoying time together and a glass of wine with family and friends. This is a slower pace and one of the most rewarding. Retirement is comfortable and a pleasant phase of our life. You can enjoy a similar outcome.

www.ingramcontent.com/pod-product-compliance
Lightning Source LLC
Chambersburg PA
CBHW030943180526
45163CB00002B/684